Introduction

Welcome!

If you are reading this, then you have already made the decision to learn to play the drums so that you can play some of your favorite popular songs. One of the best things about playing in a Modern Band is that you don't need much time to start jammin', but there are also plenty of skills to learn and master over time. This method book is designed to teach you skills to play drumset and create music in a variety of popular music styles—pop, rock, R&B, funk, hip-hop, and more!

This book is designed for you to learn with other Modern Band musicians so you can jam with your friends and classmates, but it can also be used as a stand-alone book to learn how to play the drumset. Though some of the skills that you will be working on during each section will be different from those of the other instruments, all of the Full Band Songs 🎸🥁 are designed to be played together by an entire Modern Band.

Jam Tracks 🔊 and Video Lessons ▶

Use the audio Jam Tracks throughout this book to practice the songs and exercises. Also be sure to watch the included video lessons that demonstrate many of the techniques and concepts. To access all of the audio and video files for download or streaming, just visit *www.halleonard.com/mylibrary* and enter the code found on page 1 of this book.

The Drumset

Below is a typical drumset. Your drumset might have more or fewer instruments:

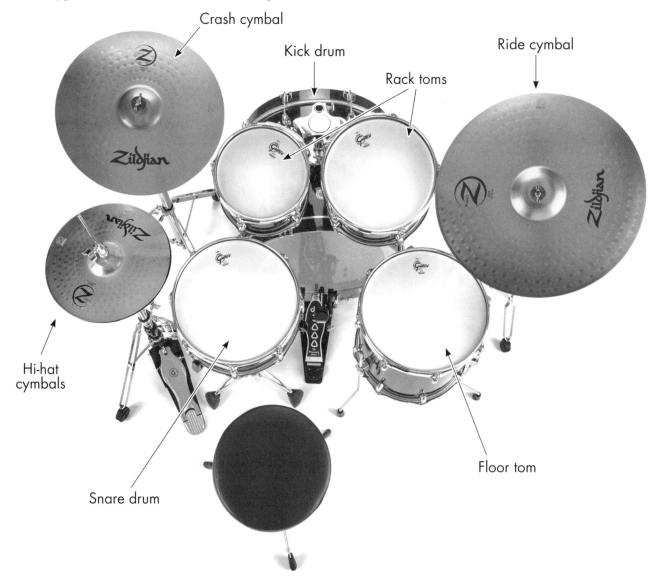

Crash cymbal

Kick drum

Rack toms

Ride cymbal

Hi-hat cymbals

Snare drum

Floor tom

Basic Technique

To hold the drumsticks, grab them between your thumb and index finger, approximately one third of the way up from the base of the stick. Then, wrap the rest of your fingers gently around the stick. Make sure you don't have any tension in your shoulders, arms, wrists, or fingers. You should always feel relaxed while playing.

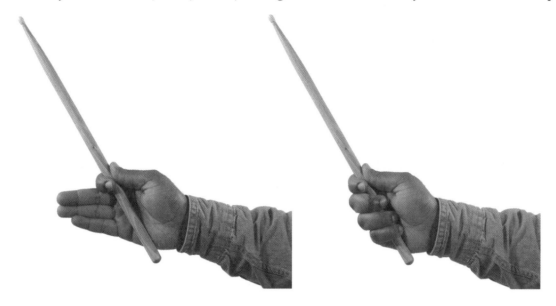

Both sticks are held the same way in each hand. This is called **matched grip**:

As a starting point, most drummers play with the right hand on the **hi-hat cymbals** and their left hand on the **snare drum**:

When it comes to using the feet, the natural placement that works along with the hand assignments is to put the right foot on the bass drum pedal and the left foot on the hi-hat pedal:

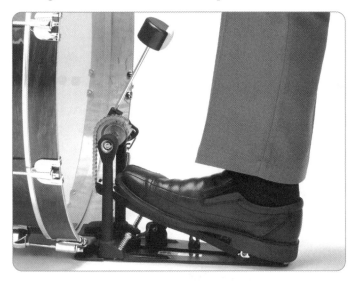 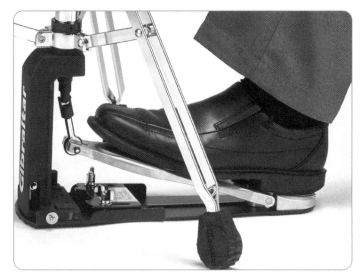

Iconic Notation

To show drum grooves, we will use **grid** or **iconic notation**. These figures, which we will call **drumbeat diagrams**, are read left to right, and the counting is written below. Anything that lines up in a vertical column is played at the same time, like the bass drum and hi-hat on beat 1. Here is an example:

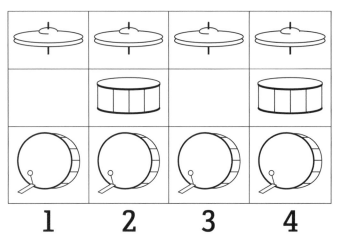

Playing in a Modern Band

When playing with a band, you should observe and listen to the rhythms and chords being played by your friends. Learning these rhythms and chords will improve your ability to comp. **Comping** means using your musical knowledge to make up rhythms and create grooves that fit a song's style.

The basic techniques and diagrams explained above will greatly help you in learning how to play the drumset. Now, let's start playing some music!

Instrument Technique: Two-Handed Drumbeat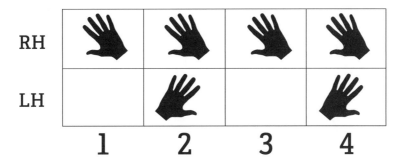

Lay the palm of your right hand on your left shoulder and pat it while counting as steady beat: "1, 2, 3, 4, 1, 2, 3, 4." Pat once for each count.

Next, add the left hand. Pat your thigh with your left hand each time you say "2" and "4". The beat will look like this:

Now, grab your drumsticks and move the pattern you just played onto the drumset to play your first drumbeat. The pictures below show the **hi-hat cymbals**, which are played with your right hand, and the **snare drum**, which is played with the left hand:

Here are the symbols we use in our drumbeat diagrams for the hi-hat and snare, respectively:

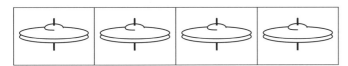

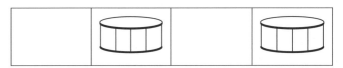

And here is the full drumbeat diagram of the pattern you played by patting your hands on your shoulder and thigh, except this time, we've used the hi-hat and snare drum symbols:

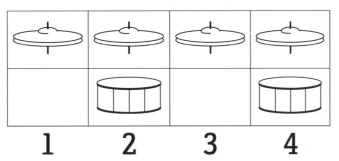

Improvisation: Switching Instruments

Now, we are ready to explore more areas of the drumset. The next two pieces are the **ride cymbal** and the **floor tom**. In the drumbeat diagram, their symbols look like this:

Move your right hand to the ride cymbal and your left hand to the floor tom, and then play the same pattern you previously used for the hi-hat and snare drum. You can try this with any two instruments on your drumset:

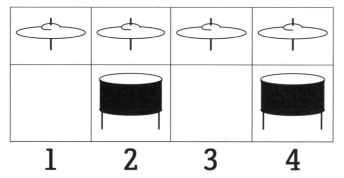

Music Theory: Doubling the Hi-Hat

When you play drums, you will often play the hi-hat cymbals closed. This means that your left foot will hold the hi-hat pedal down in the closed position, keeping the two cymbals close together to play a short sound.

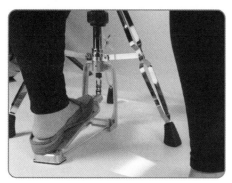  

Closed hi-hat pedal *Closed hi-hat* *Open hi-hat*

Try playing the hi-hat twice as fast now. Count "1, 2, 3, 4," but this time, add an "and" in between the numbers. We use a "+" sign to represent "and" in the drumbeat diagram. Count "1 + 2 + 3 + 4 +..." out loud as you play:

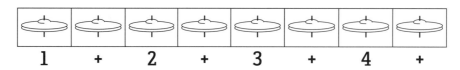

Now, add your snare drum hits back to the groove on beats 2 and 4:

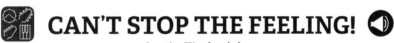

You can play this drumbeat with the songs that follow, even though what you hear on the Jam Tracks will differ from what is written in the diagram above. You'll also notice that each of these songs feature lyrics with letters written above certain words. This is called a **chord chart**. Your friends playing guitar, bass, and keyboard use this type of music to know when to switch chords. We've included the same for you so that if you are singing, then you can see the harmony change with the lyrics.

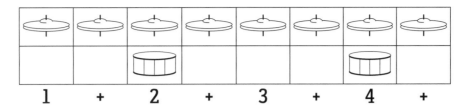

CAN'T STOP THE FEELING!
Justin Timberlake

          G   **Emi**
I've got this feeling inside my bones.

     C   **Emi**
It goes electric, wavy when I turn it on.

          G   **Emi**
All through my city, all through my home,

     C   **Emi**
We're flying up, no ceiling, when we in our zone.

          G   **Emi**
I got that sunshine in my pocket, got that good soul in my feet.

     C   **Emi**
I feel that hot blood in my body when it drops, ooh.

    G   **Emi**
I can't take my eyes up off it, moving so phenomenally.

     C   **Emi**
Room on lock the way we rock it, so don't stop.

WITHOUT YOU
David Guetta ft. Usher

G   **C**   **Emi**   **C**
I can't win, I can't reign. I will never win this game without you, without you.

G   **C**   **Emi**   **C**
I am lost, I am vain. I will never be the same without you, without you.

G   **C**   **Emi**   **C**
I won't run, I won't fly. I will never make it by without you, without you.

G   **C**   **Emi**   **C**
I can't rest, I can't fight. All I need is you and I, without you, without you.

WAKE ME UP

Avicii ft. John Legend

| Emi | C | G |
Feeling my way through the darkness,

| Emi | C | G |
Guided by a beating heart.

| Emi | C | G |
I can't tell where the journey will end,

| Emi | C | G |
But I know where to start.

| Emi | C | G |
They tell me I'm too young to understand.

| Emi | C | G |
They say I'm caught up in a dream.

| Emi | C | G |
Well, life will pass me by if I don't open up my eyes.

| Emi | C | G |
Well, that's fine by me.

| Emi | C | G |
So wake me up when it's all over,

| Emi | C | G |
When I'm wiser and I'm older.

| Emi | C | G |
All this time I was finding myself

| Emi | C | G |
And I didn't know I was lost.

Words and Music by Aloe Blacc, Tim Bergling and Michael Einziger
Copyright © 2011, 2013 Aloe Blacc Publishing, Inc., EMI Music Publishing Scandinavia AB, Universal Music Corp. and Elementary Particle Music
All Rights for Aloe Blacc Publishing, Inc. Administered Worldwide by Kobalt Songs Music Publishing
All Rights for EMI Music Publishing Scandinavia AB Administered by Sony/ATV Music Publishing LLC, 424 Church Street, Suite 1200, Nashville, TN 37219
All Rights for Elementary Particle Music Administered by Universal Music Corp.
All Rights Reserved   Used by Permission

SEND MY LOVE (TO YOUR NEW LOVER)

Adele

G
This was all you, none of it me. You put your hands on, on my body and told me, Emi

you told me you were ready

G
For the big one, for the big jump. I'd be your last love, everlasting, you and me. Emi

That was what you told me.

G   Emi
I'm giving you up, I've forgiven it all. You set me free.

G
Send my love to your new lover, treat her better.

Emi
We've gotta let go of all of our ghosts. We both know we ain't kids no more.

G
Send my love to your new lover, treat her better.

Emi
We've gotta let go of all of our ghosts.

We both know we ain't kids no more.

Words and Music by Adele Adkins, Max Martin and Shellback
Copyright © 2015 MELTED STONE PUBLISHING LTD. and MXM
All Rights for MELTED STONE PUBLISHING LTD. in the U.S. and Canada
Administered by UNIVERSAL - SONGS OF POLYGRAM INTERNATIONAL, INC.
All Rights for MXM Administered Worldwide by KOBALT SONGS MUSIC PUBLISHING
All Rights Reserved   Used by Permission

Composition

Great drummers are also composers. This means that they can write their own drumbeats. Rewrite the drumbeat you've already learned here:

1. Write out your steady, right-hand beat, and add the notes played on the snare drum on beats 2 and 4:

2. Now, you can add in one extra snare drum beat wherever you would like. Below is a grid if you want to write another:

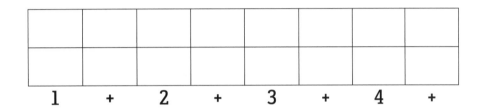

3. You can now practice your new groove!

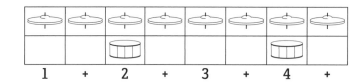

Form of Recording: Intro–Chorus–Verse–Chorus–Verse–Chorus

You can play the drumbeat you just learned throughout the entire song:

CHORUS

```
        G                          C
I gotta feeling that tonight's gonna be a good night,

             Emi                              C
That tonight's gonna be a good night, that tonight's gonna be a good, good night.
```

VERSE

```
G                          C
Tonight's the night, let's live it up. I got my money, let's spend it up.

Emi                             C
Go out and smash it, like, oh my God. Jump off that sofa, let's get, get off.
```

VERSE

```
G                          C
I know that we'll have a ball if we get down and go out and just lose it all.

       Emi                          C
I feel stressed out, I wanna let go. Let's go way out, spaced out, and losing all control.
```

VERSE

```
G                          C
Fill up my cup, Mazel Tov! Look at her dancing, just take it off.

Emi
Let's paint the town, we'll shut it down.

    C
Let's burn the roof, and then we'll do it again.
```

Going Beyond: Singing and Playing

Another important skill for a musician is to be able to both play your instrument and sing. Here are a few basic tips for singing and playing:

- Make sure you have your drumbeat learned well enough so that you can play it without thinking about your coordination. Then, try speaking the lyrics (in rhythm) over it.
- Sing the lyrics while playing steady notes on the hi-hat.
- Don't worry too much about singing the correct pitches at this point; just practice the skill of doing two things at once.

SECTION 2

Playing Drumbeats

To warm-up, play the drumbeat below along to the song "Low Rider" by War:

LOW RIDER
War

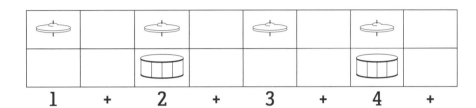

Instrument Technique: The Kick Drum

Now that you can play the drumbeat with your hands, add in the **kick drum**. The kick drum is also known as the **bass drum**. Here is the symbol we will use in our drumbeat diagram:

Try these beats using the kick drum and the snare drum:

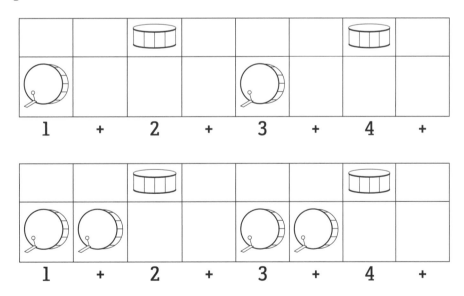

You can use this same beat to play "We Will Rock You" by Queen. Drumbeats rarely stay exactly the same throughout a whole song, so listen to each song carefully to find any variations.

WE WILL ROCK YOU
Queen

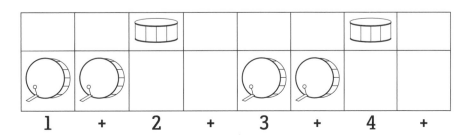

Putting Three Instruments Together ▶

To play three instruments at the same time, you can start by playing your hi-hat on beats 1, 2, 3, and 4, your kick drum on beats 1 and 3, and your snare drum on beats 2 and 4:

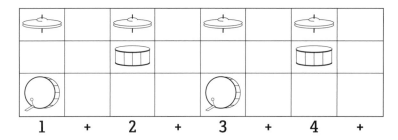

You can work up to this by playing just two parts at a time. Start with just the kick and snare:

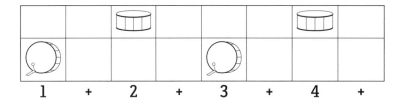

Now, try just the bass drum with the hi-hat:

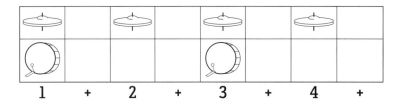

You can now put it all back together. Start slow to make sure everything is played at the correct point in time:

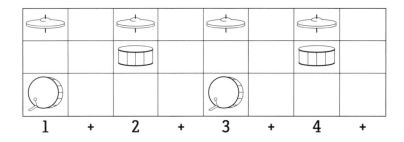

When you're ready, double the speed of your hi-hat by playing "1 + 2 + 3 + 4 +." Again, start with just two instruments and go slowly to make sure you're playing accurately:

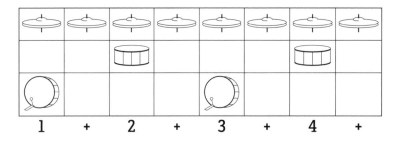

The drumbeat we just played features something that we call a **backbeat**. A backbeat refers to a groove that emphasizes beats 2 and 4, usually played on the snare drum. As you listen and play along, try playing the hi-hat on "1, 2, 3, 4" or "1 + 2 + 3 + 4 +" with the snare drum backbeat and see which sounds better:

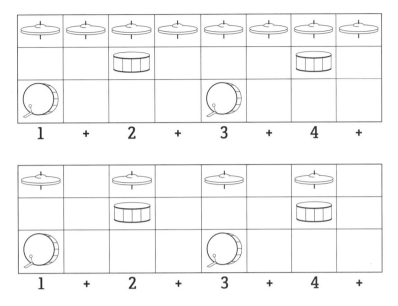

Instrument Technique: Heel Up and Heel Down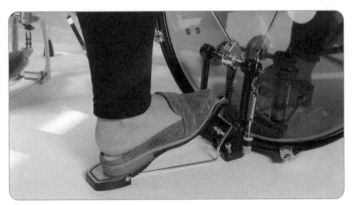

There are two common ways to play your kick drum:

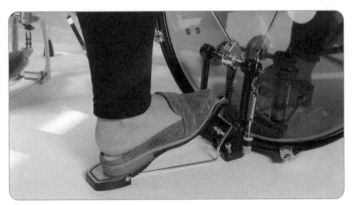 

Both techniques are correct. Pick the one that works best for you. You might want to use different techniques depending on the music you are playing.

Music Theory: Quarter and Eighth Notes

When you played the hi-hat only on the beats, you were playing **quarter notes**:

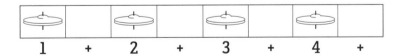

Using **standard notation**, that rhythm played in the drumbeat diagram above can be written like this:

When you played the hi-hat on "1 + 2 + 3 + 4 +," you were playing **eighth notes**:

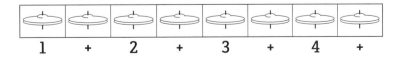

This rhythm can be written like this in standard notation:

Playing Drumbeats: Applying the Backbeat

The backbeat we played previously is used in songs such as "Love On Top" by Beyoncé:

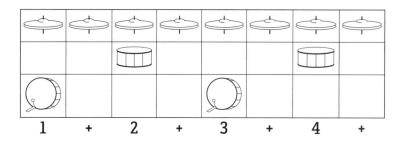

This beat is used in songs such as the verse from "Dynamite" by Taio Cruz:

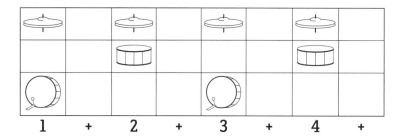

Drumbeat Variations: Playing the Crash Cymbal

It's now time to introduce another piece of the drumset: the **crash cymbal**. We use this symbol in our drumbeat diagram:

Here is a picture showing where the crash cymbal is usually placed in a drumset configuration:

The crash cymbal is often played on beat 1 at the beginning of a section of music. You can play the crash instead of the hi-hat on that particular beat:

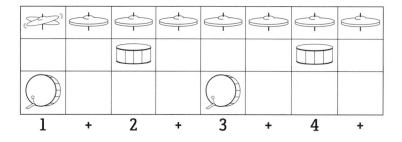

16

If you want to simplify that beat, then play this variation:

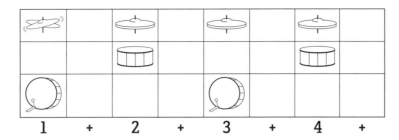

Music Theory: Using Your Ears and Your Voice

In "Heathens" by Twenty One Pilots, the drummer plays a backbeat with one bass drum hit moved away from beat 3. Here's a drumbeat diagram with the second bass drum beat removed:

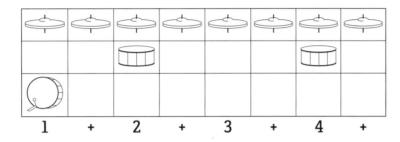

Beatboxing to Transcribe ▶

Transcribing music is a big part of being a musician, and drummers often use **beatboxing** to learn parts from a recording. Beatboxing is a way that you can use your voice to replicate the sounds of the drumset. You can use the words "boots" (bass drum) and "cats" (snare drum) to beatbox drum sounds. You can make them sound better by emphasizing the beginning of each word and not pronouncing the end. The sounds will be more like "buh" and "kah."

Can you beatbox to find where the removed bass drum beat goes in "Heathens?"
1. Listen to the recording, and try beatboxing just the bass and snare drum.
2. Try counting the beats out loud. The bass drum comes after which number?
3. Write where you hear the kick drum in the drumbeat diagram below.

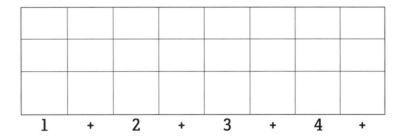

Does your drumbeat look like this one?

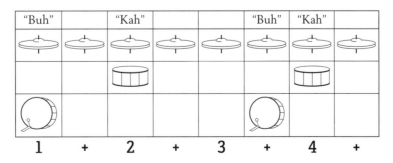

You will use this beat in the Full Band Song "Heathens" by Twenty One Pilots.

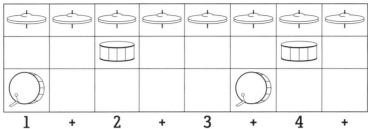
Form of Recording: Chorus–Verse–Chorus–Verse–Chorus–Chorus

Drumbeat

1	+	2	+	3	+	4	+

CHORUS

```
C           Ami          E    C           Ami          E
```
All my friends are heathens, take it slow. Wait for them to ask you who you know.

```
    C           Ami        E       C           Ami          E
```
Please don't make any sudden moves. You don't know the half of the abuse.

VERSE

```
C
```
Welcome to the room of people who have rooms of people

```
        Emi
```
that they loved one day docked away.

```
Ami
```
Just because we check the guns at the door doesn't mean

```
        Emi
```
our brains will change from hand grenades.

```
C                   Ami                Emi
```
You'll never know the psychopath sitting next to you.

You'll never know the murderer sitting next to you.

```
C                   Ami              B
```
You'll think, "How'd I get here, sitting next to you?"

But after all I've said, please don't forget.

SECTION 3

Instrument Technique: Slow Backbeat

There are many ways to write music. One way is to use **staff notation**.
The **staff** is made up of five lines and four spaces:

The drums are part of the percussion family, so the staff uses a **percussion** or **neutral clef**
at the beginning of every system:

The symbols on this staff (called **noteheads**) each represent an instrument on the drumset. Since each note in the following examples lasts for one beat of music, they are all quarter notes. These notes represent the kick drum:

These represent the snare:

And these X-shaped noteheads represent the hi-hat:

Here is a new symbol that is called a **quarter rest**; this simply means that instead of playing, you'll rest for one quarter note value: ⧙ You can also combine two quarter rests into one **half rest**: ▬

Slow the quarter note backbeat down to play this '70s rock tune:

DAZED AND CONFUSED 🔊
Led Zeppelin

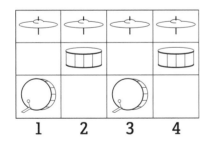

These symbols are called **repeat signs**; they're used to tell the player to repeat the music contained between the symbols:

The eighth-note backbeat that you previously played looks like this:

19

Playing Drumbeats: Backbeat Variation

Play a backbeat, but this time, play the ride cymbal instead of the hi-hat. The following example uses the ride cymbal, which is placed on the top line of the staff. All cymbals are written with X-shaped noteheads.

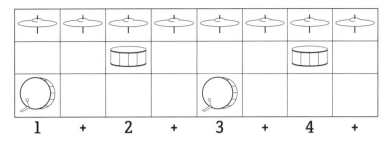 

Here are some songs with drum parts that either use a backbeat or a slight variation:

IMAGINE
John Lennon

This example has eighth notes in the kick drum line:

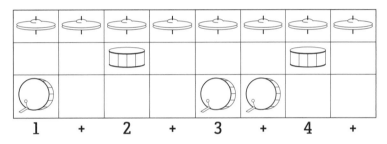 

This example has eighth notes in the snare drum:

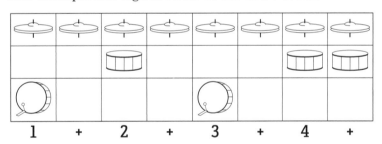 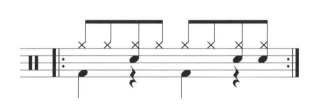

In the next song, we've simplified the groove in the drumbeat diagram and notation compared to what you'll hear in the Jam Track. Feel free to replicate the additional bass drum part on your own after you've mastered what we've written for you!

BEST DAY OF MY LIFE
American Authors

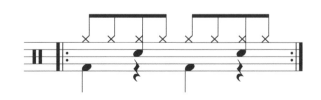

Instrument Technique: Playing the Hi-Hat

Depending on how much you lift your foot from the hi-hat pedal, the sound will be tighter or looser. To play a "tight" or "closed" hi-hat, keep your foot firmly planted on the hi-hat pedal. The hi-hat cymbal should look like this:

Tight (closed)

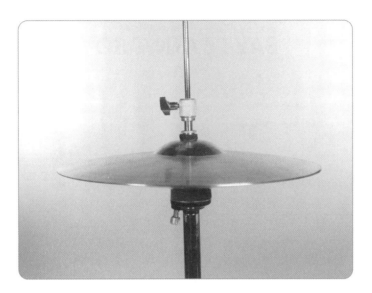

The symbol that we've used in our drumbeat diagrams so far is the one that we will now use for the closed hi-hat:

The following example shows the notehead used to notate a closed hi-hat. It simply places a "+" sign above the note:

To play a "loose" or "half-open" hi-hat, lift up your left foot from the hi-hat pedal. The picture below shows the cymbals placed slightly open, but not all the way:

Loose (half-open)

This is the symbol we will use in our drumbeat diagrams for the loose hi-hat:

This is the notehead used to notate the open hi-hat, over which a small circle is placed above the note:

If you see a measure of hi-hat noteheads with no symbols written above them, then assume that they will be played closed. If there are mixed open and closed hi-hats within the same measure, then the appropriate symbols will appear above each notehead.

Here are some songs that feature drumbeats with open and closed hi-hats in different sections. The first drumbeat features a symbol called an **eighth rest**. It functions just like the quarter rest, but for the value of one eighth note: ⅞

SAY IT AIN'T SO
Weezer

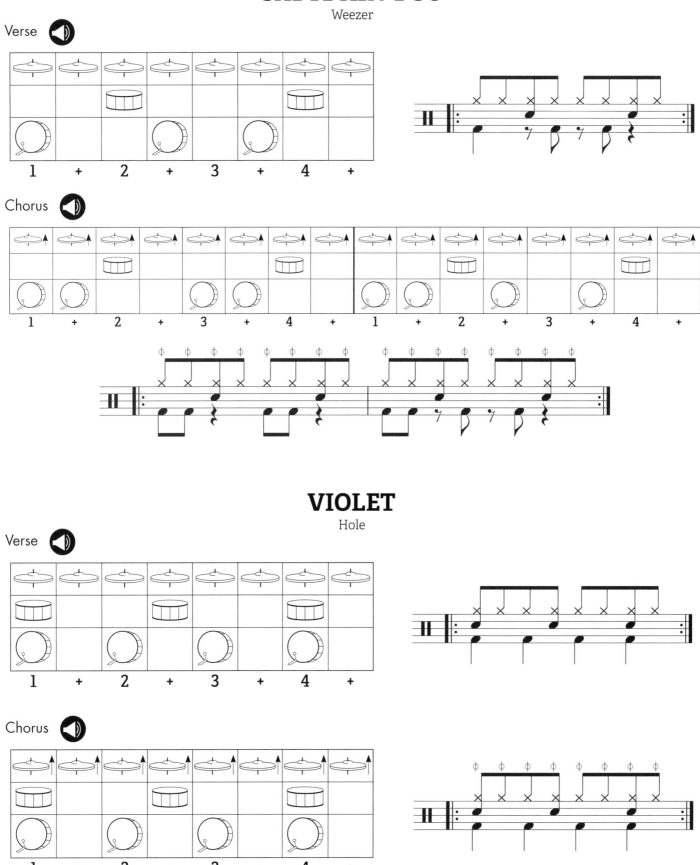

VIOLET
Hole

Music Theory: Form

Here is an example of a song that changes grooves between the Verse and Chorus:

SEVEN NATION ARMY
The White Stripes

The Verse looks like this:

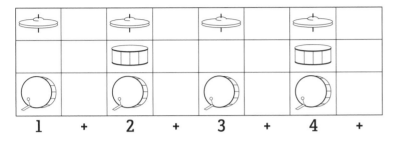

During the Chorus, play the ride cymbal instead of the hi-hat (don't be afraid to dig in!):

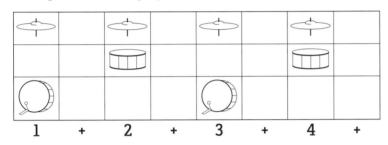

Remember when you practiced playing the crash on beat 1? You can use this to signify a new section of a song, such as a chorus or verse. Playing the crash and bass drum together on beat 1 is commonly used to introduce new song sections. The following example shows the symbol used for the crash cymbal as it appears in standard staff notation. It uses a symbol called a **ledger line**; ledger lines are used to show notes that appear above or below the standard five-line staff:

ROAR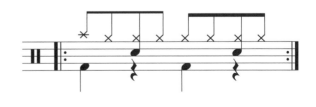
Katy Perry

The different cymbals show up on separate lines in staff notation:

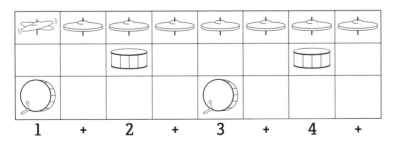

On songs like "Radioactive" by Imagine Dragons and "Come as You Are" by Nirvana, you can use a crash on beat 1 of a new section to signify the change.

Composition: Verse and Chorus

Let's practice writing grooves for our own original songs. Write a groove to be used for the verse, and then change it slightly for the chorus. Don't veer too far from the backbeat, but feel free to move a kick drum or snare drum hit to make it your own. You might also want to switch to different cymbals or drums to add variety.

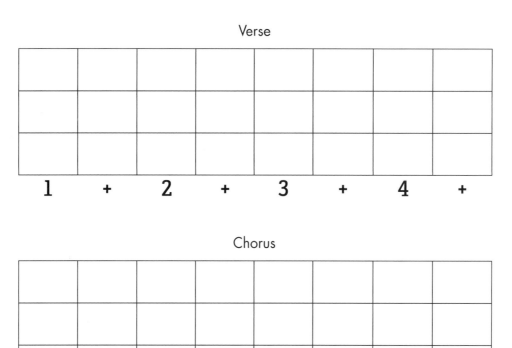

Instrument Technique: Different Kick Drum Patterns

Play through these few drum patterns as a warm-up:

KIDS
MGMT

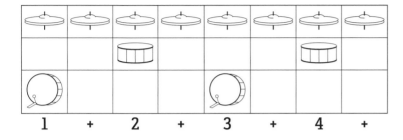

UNDER PRESSURE
Queen ft. David Bowie

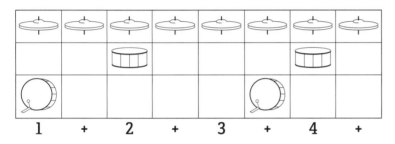

HOLD ON
Alabama Shakes

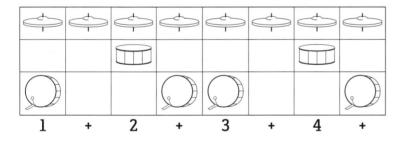

Playing Drumbeats: Drum Fills

Fills accent something that's happening in the music, usually a change in form or melody. They tend to lead up to a new section and often end on beat 1 with a crash and kick. The following examples show different kinds of fills. Keep in mind that each suggested rhythm could be played on any combination of instruments. This section also introduces a new instrument, the **rack tom**:

Here's the symbol that we'll use in our drumbeat diagrams:

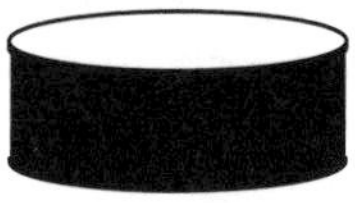

The following fills are labeled according to where they are played within the measure:

"4 + 1" Fills

Example 1

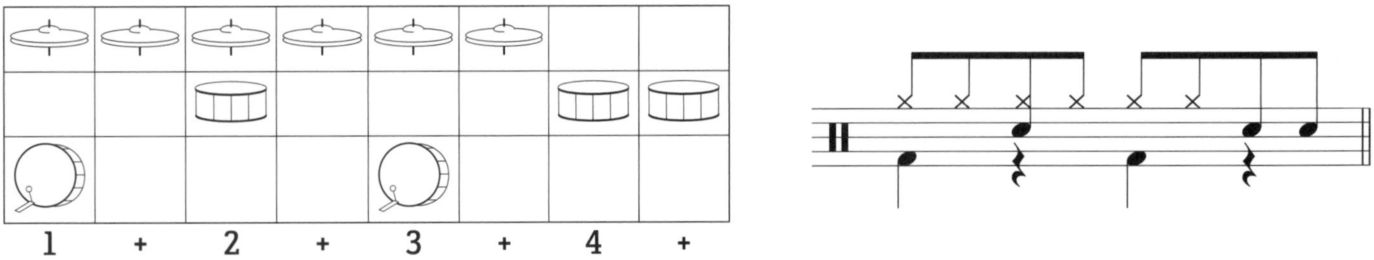

Example 2

The eighth notes here are split between three instruments:

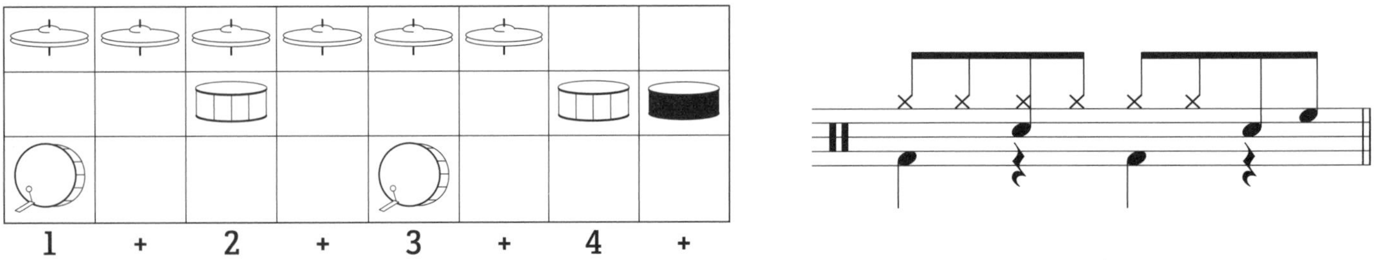

3 + 4 + 1 Fills

Example 3

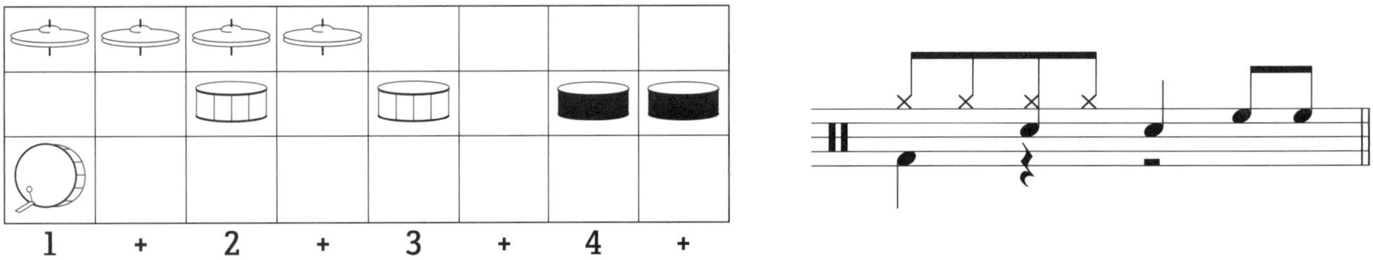

Example 4

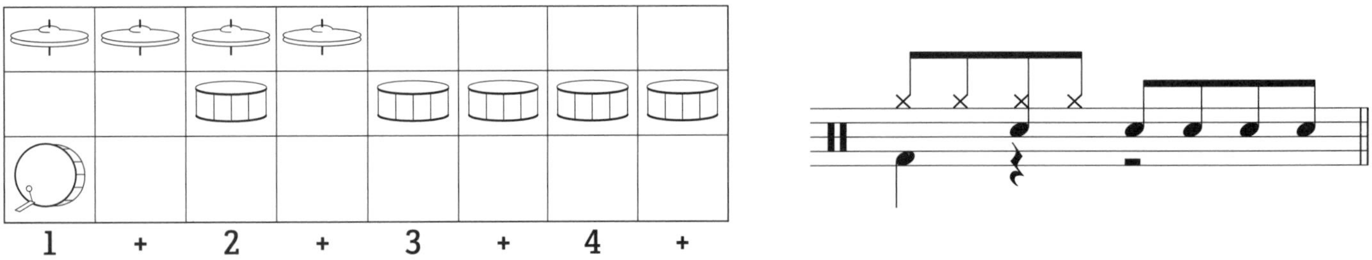

Example 5

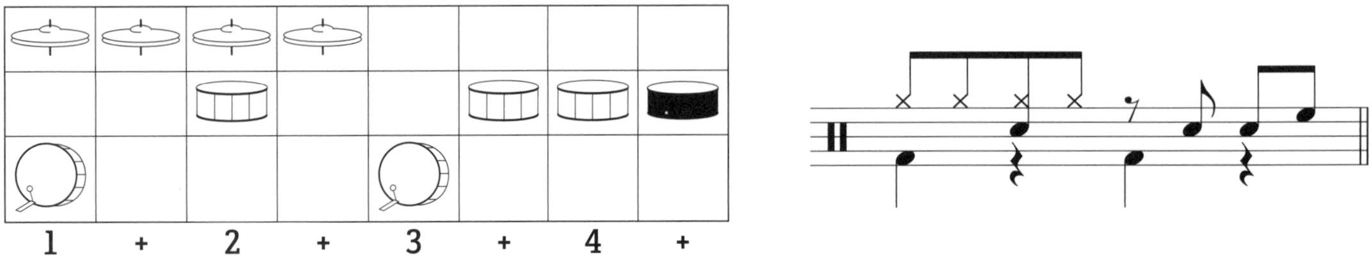

Music Theory: Sixteenth Notes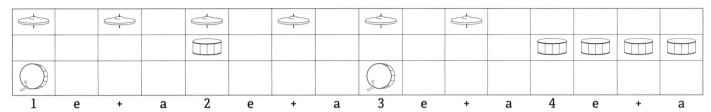

In this next example, there are four evenly played notes on the snare drum during beat 4. These are called **sixteenth notes**. They are counted "1–e–and–a, 2–e–and–a…":

They are written like this in staff notation:

The drumbeat diagram from above looks like this in standard staff notation:

Instrument Technique: Applying Drumbeats and Adding Fills

Here are a few more drumbeats you can play with your bandmates. Try adding a fill here or there into these songs.

WE WILL ROCK YOU
Queen

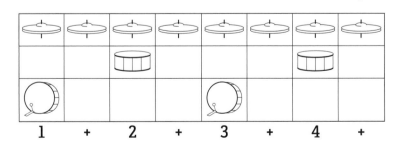

BACK IN BLACK
AC/DC

WHAT MAKES YOU BEAUTIFUL

One Direction

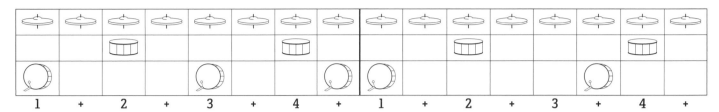

Composition: Writing Lyrics ▶

Here are three steps you can take to help you write lyrics:

- Pick a theme: Lyrics can be easy to write when you have something you want to say. Think of something you care about and write based on that, such as friends, family, hobbies, or dreams.
- Choose two words that rhyme, such as "great" and "late" or "thrill" and "chill." Then, choose another pair of words.
- Turn your paired words into sentences, and then try to speak the words in rhythm and sing along with the Jam Track. Here is an example of a verse for a song written about songwriting:

Writing	lyrics	is	so	fun,	can	be	done	by	any - one.
/	/	/	/		/	/	/	/	

Think	of	what	to	write	a - bout;	play	some	chords, and	sing	or	shout!
/	/	/	/		/	/	/	/	

Write a Drum Fill

Write your own drum fills that lead to beat 1, using eighth notes or sixteenth notes:

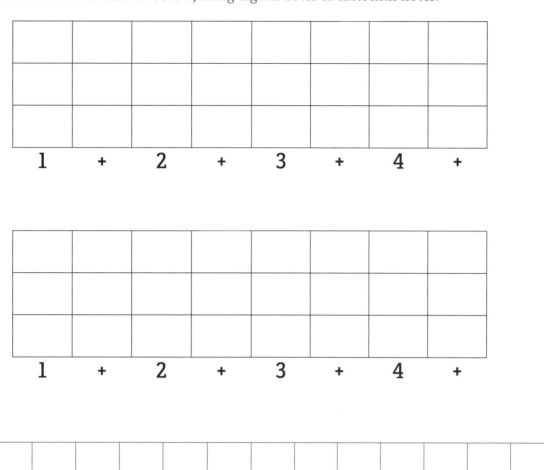

1   +   2   +   3   +   4   +

1   +   2   +   3   +   4   +

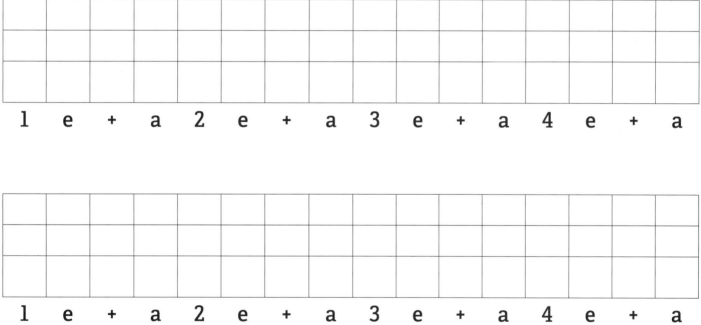

1 e + a 2 e + a 3 e + a 4 e + a

1 e + a 2 e + a 3 e + a 4 e + a

Fills are fun to play, but playing them too often can cover up what your bandmates are doing. Fills should be used only for specific reasons, such as switching to a new section of a song.

Bob Marley & the Wailers

Form of Recording: Intro–Chorus–Verse–Chorus–Verse–Chorus

This tune features a **reggae one-drop** beat (more on this in Section 8). In this pattern, the kick drum and snare drum play together on beats 2 and 4:

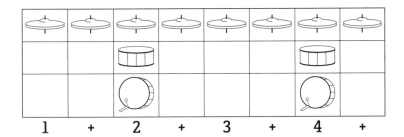 

CHORUS

A   D   E   A   D   E
Stir it up. Little darlin', stir it up. Come on, baby.

              A   D   E   A   D   E
Come on and stir it up. Little darlin', stir it up. O-oh!

VERSE

    A   D
It's been a long, long time, yeah (stir it, stir it, stir it together).

E   A   D   E
Since I got you on my mind (ooh-ooh-ooh-ooh).

A   D   E
Now you are here (stir it, stir it, stir it together). I said, it's so clear.

   A   D   E
To see what we could do, baby (ooh-ooh-ooh-ooh). Just me and you.

SECTION 5

Instrument Technique: Rudiments ▶

Rudiments are the building blocks of drumming. They are patterns assigned to the right and left hands that can change the **articulation** (how a note is first sounded or struck) of a note along with helping you navigate the drumset as your grooves become more complex. Play this fill by alternating your right and left hands on sixteenth notes, starting on beat 3:

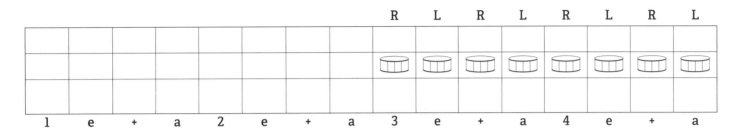

Fills like this are used in songs like "Day Tripper" by the Beatles.

Practicing rudiments is a great way to build up your musical vocabulary so that you can play more of the ideas that you hear, eventually using them to play solos or grooves. There are many rudiments, but here are three of the most common ones. Practice these on the snare drum in time with a metronome or with a Jam Track:

Singles

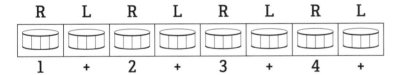

Doubles

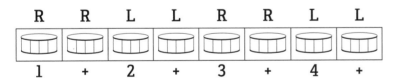

Paradiddles

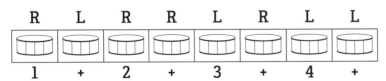

Instrument Technique: The Hi-Hat Pedal

You can also play singles, doubles, and paradiddles with your feet. Practice these with your kick drum and hi-hat pedal, in time with a metronome or a Jam Track. The hi-hat pedal is played with your left foot, so it's placed on the bottom of the staff. Since it's a cymbal, it's written with an X-shaped notehead:

Here is the symbol we'll use for the hi-hat played with the foot pedal in our drumbeat diagrams:

Singles

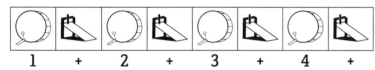

Doubles

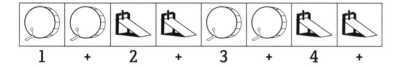

Paradiddles

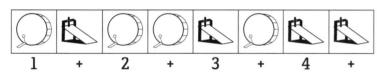

Playing Drumbeats: Playing with Bass

CRUEL
St. Vincent

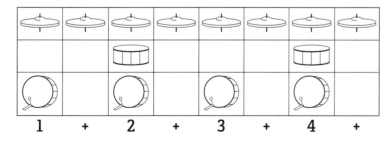 

Notice how the bass drum plays on all four downbeats in this groove. The bass guitar is playing the same rhythm, so make sure that your kick drum lines up with the bass guitar.

Many drum grooves are similar to each other, but their subtle differences can make a big difference in how the overall groove comes together. These drumbeats, one of which you've already played, are great examples of this:

SAY IT AIN'T SO (Verse)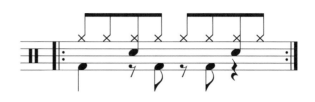
Weezer

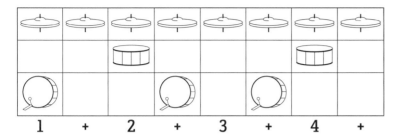

FREE FALLIN'
Tom Petty

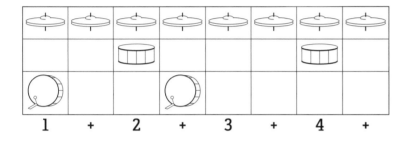

In a great band, all the players pay close attention to what their bandmates are playing. For bassists, listening to the drummer is especially important. Together, the bass and drums tell the rest of the band important information about tempo, rhythm, style, and note lengths. In this section, you will practice playing some examples of the bass guitar-kick drum connection in music. With that in mind, try two more examples:

DOO WOP (THAT THING)
Lauryn Hill

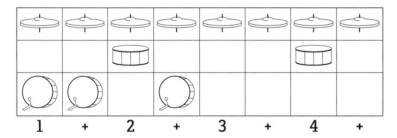

YOU KNOW I'M NO GOOD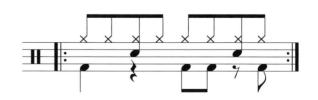
Amy Winehouse

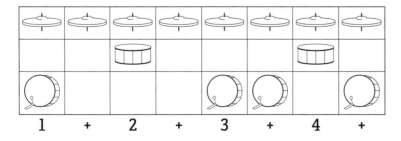

Composition: Mastering the Grid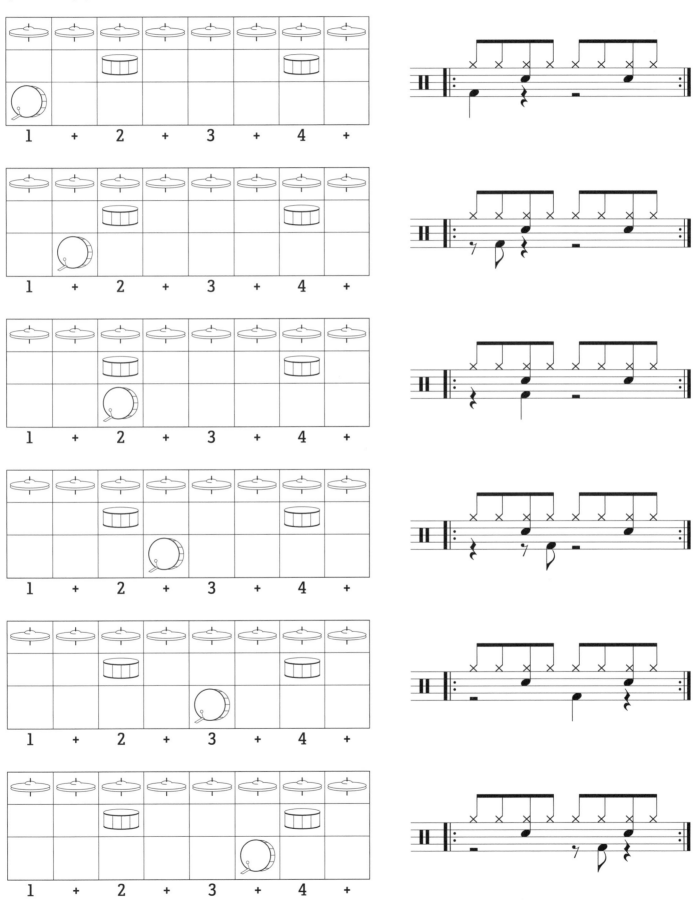

Now that you've played several examples of grooves where the bass drum and bass guitar play the same rhythms, try writing some of your own. First, see what all the options are on this eighth-note grid. When you first start this, play eighth notes on your hi-hat as you play the bass drum hits with your right foot. Then, add in the snare drum backbeat as well. When writing these in staff notation, you can see where the noteheads line up vertically, just like in the drumbeat diagram. You can practice these grooves together with a bass player:

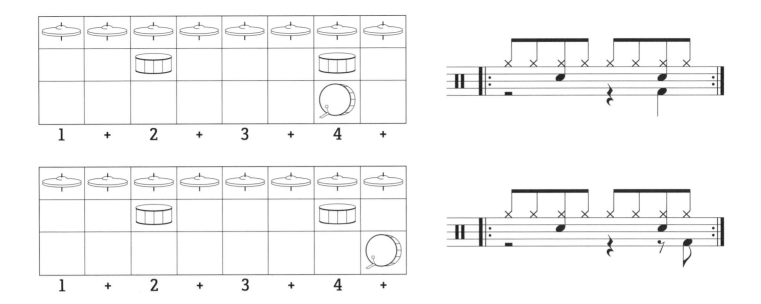

Use the grids below to come up with a rhythm that you and the bass player can play together:

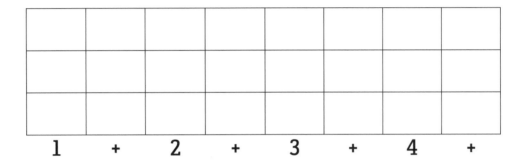

It doesn't have to be the bass drum that lines up with the bass guitar. You could mix up the bass drum with the snare drum to play rhythms that fit in with the bass line. Try that with another drumbeat, and write your ideas in this diagram below:

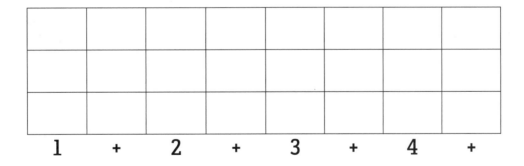

Closing Thought

As you listen to more music with this bass guitar-kick drum relationship in mind, you'll notice that many of the rhythms don't line up together exactly, but they **accent** (emphasize) certain notes together (more on accents later in the book).

SECTION 6

Playing Drumbeats: Placing the Crashes

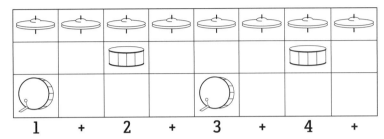

Wilson Pickett

If you're playing with your bandmates, then this a great opportunity to lock in with the bassist. You may also want to use the crash cymbal from time to time to reinforce accented points in the music:

Staff notation is especially helpful for showing longer examples of music. Where is the crash cymbal played in the example below? Play this with your bandmates in "Land of a Thousand Dances":

Instrument Technique: Dynamics

The beat of this song doesn't change much throughout, so how do you keep the music interesting? This is where we can use **dynamics** to add variety within the song. Dynamics are how loud or soft you play. Using a variety of dynamics is a great way to make different sections of the form stand out from each other. For "Life Is a Highway," you can play at a softer dynamic on the Verses and a louder dynamic on the Chorus. You can generally control the volume of your playing with the height of your drumstick:

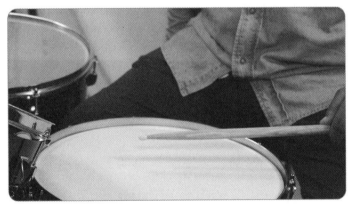

For softer sounds, position the tip of your stick closer to the drumhead.

For louder sounds, position the tip of your stick higher above the drumhead.

Here is a drumbeat that is used in songs like "Life Is a Highway" as recorded by the country band Rascal Flatts; you can vary your dynamics in the different sections of the song.

LIFE IS A HIGHWAY

Rascal Flatts

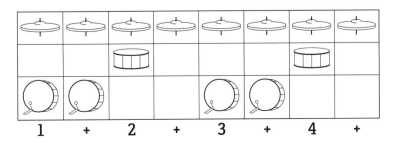

Long Sounds vs. Short Sounds

Each piece in the drumset is made to be played just about anywhere regarding the different surfaces of the drumheads and areas of the cymbals. Experiment with your drumset and find which drums, cymbals, rims, etc., make the shortest sounds and which ones ring out for longer sounds. Each of these sounds has a marking in staff notation.

Examples of Longer Sounds:

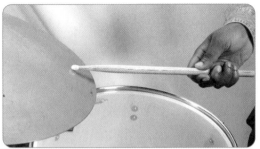

Ride cymbal near the edge

Un-muffled floor tom

Loose hi-hat

Examples of Shorter Sounds:

Ride cymbal bell

Snare drum (especially in the middle)

Closed hi-hat

Changing Instrumentation

Because you have access to all these different sounds on your instrument, you can often change a drumbeat slightly by switching out one or more sounds with something similar. Here are some examples that switch out the hi-hat for the floor tom:

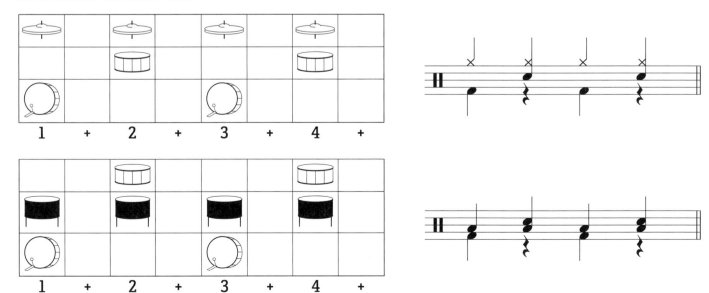

These drumbeats are used in songs such as "Holiday" by Green Day:

HOLIDAY
Green Day

Intro/Interlude

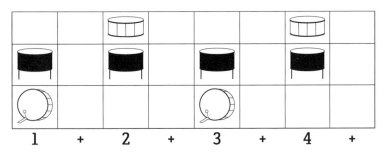

Verse

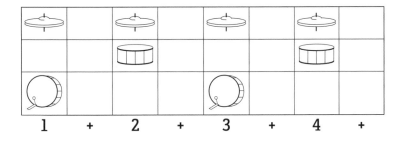

Chorus

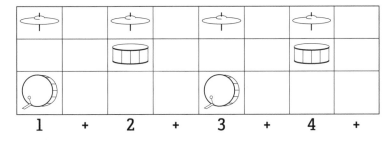

The next sound we'll discuss is the **rim click**. Rim clicks are shown by replacing the regular notehead with an X. We'll use this symbol in our drumbeat diagrams to show rim clicks:

Here is a song that uses rim clicks:

AIN'T IT FUN
Paramore

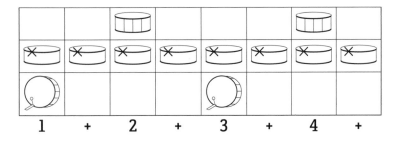

Instrument Technique: Double-Stroke Rolls

A **double-stroke roll** combines several short sounds to make an overall longer sound. This technique takes practice, so start slow and have fun with it. On each snare drum hit, let the stick bounce and hit the drumhead one more time. So in one motion, the stick will hit the head of the drum twice.

Improvisation: Using Rudiments in Solos ▶

Using the rudiments (singles, doubles, and paradiddles) you learned in Section 5, play some of these rhythms. First, use only your hands. The later exercises combine hands and feet. Later, you can practice adding in your double-stroke rolls. Standard staff notation can be especially helpful when there are multiple instruments.

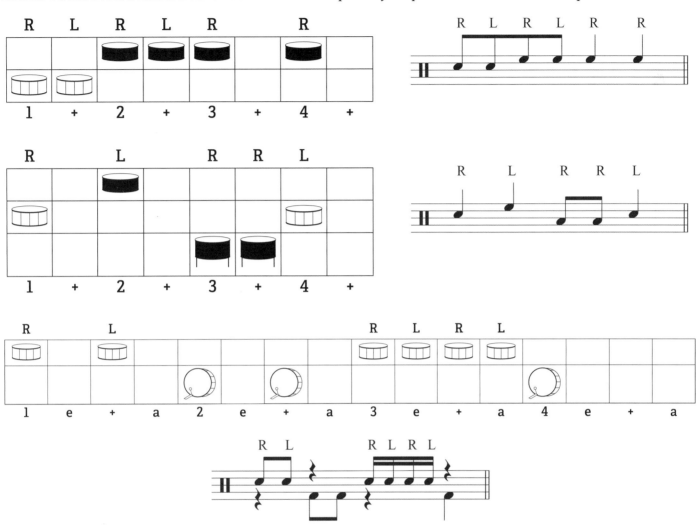

As you start creating your own rhythms, keep in mind that you can change your rhythm, instrumentation, and dynamics as much as you want. Put on any Jam Track and try soloing along.

Full Band Song: SOMEONE LIKE YOU 🔊
Adele

Form of Recording: Intro–Verse–Pre-Chorus–Chorus–Verse–Pre-Chorus–Chorus–Bridge–Chorus
This song originally has no drum track, but this doesn't mean you shouldn't play with your bandmates when you perform this song. Instead, think about everything you've learned so far. What would be the best sounds to use on this song? Are there any parts you could accent? Should your drumbeat be the same in the Verse and Chorus? Create your drum chart using the grids below:

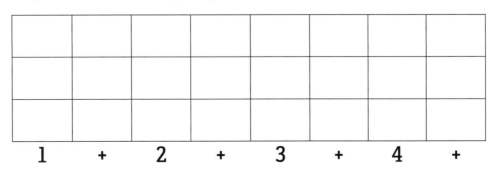

Suggestions

We've included some suggested drumbeats for you to use. You can listen to the Jam Track for inspiration; we used various approaches in our recorded version.

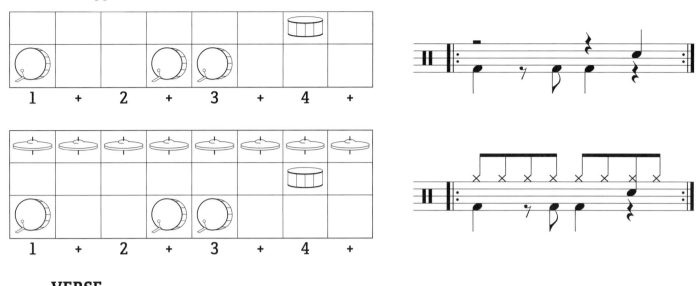

VERSE

```
G                    D                  Emi                    C
```
I heard that you're settled down, that you found a girl and you're married now.
```
G                    D                        Emi                 C
```
I heard that your dreams came true. Guess she gave you things I didn't give to you.
```
G                    D              Emi                    C
```
Old friend, why are you so shy? Ain't like you to hold back or hide from the light.

PRE-CHORUS

```
D                      Emi                C
```
I hate to turn up out of the blue uninvited, but I couldn't stay away, I couldn't fight it.
```
D                    Emi                              C
```
I had hoped you'd see my face and that you'd be reminded that for me it isn't over.

CHORUS

```
G              D          Emi          C
```
Never mind, I'll find someone like you.
```
        G              D          Emi          C
```
I wish nothing but the best for you two.
```
G            D          Emi          C
```
Don't forget me, I beg. I'll remember you said,
```
        G              D                  Emi          C
```
"Sometimes it lasts in love, but sometimes it hurts instead,
```
        G              D                  Emi          C
```
Sometimes it lasts in love, but sometimes it hurts instead."

BRIDGE

```
D
```
Nothing compares, no worries or cares,
```
     Emi
```
Regrets and mistakes, they're memories made.
```
C                                      Ami  G        C          D
```
Who would have known how bittersweet this would taste?

Words and Music by Adele Adkins and Dan Wilson
Copyright © 2011 MELTED STONE PUBLISHING LTD., BMG MONARCH and SUGAR LAKE MUSIC
All Rights for MELTED STONE PUBLISHING LTD. in the U.S. and Canada Controlled and
Administered by UNIVERSAL - SONGS OF POLYGRAM INTERNATIONAL, INC.
All Rights for BMG MONARCH and SUGAR LAKE MUSIC
Administered by BMG RIGHTS MANAGEMENT (US) LLC
All Rights Reserved   Used by Permission

SECTION 7

Warm-Up

Try reading these examples in both drumbeat diagrams and staff notation:

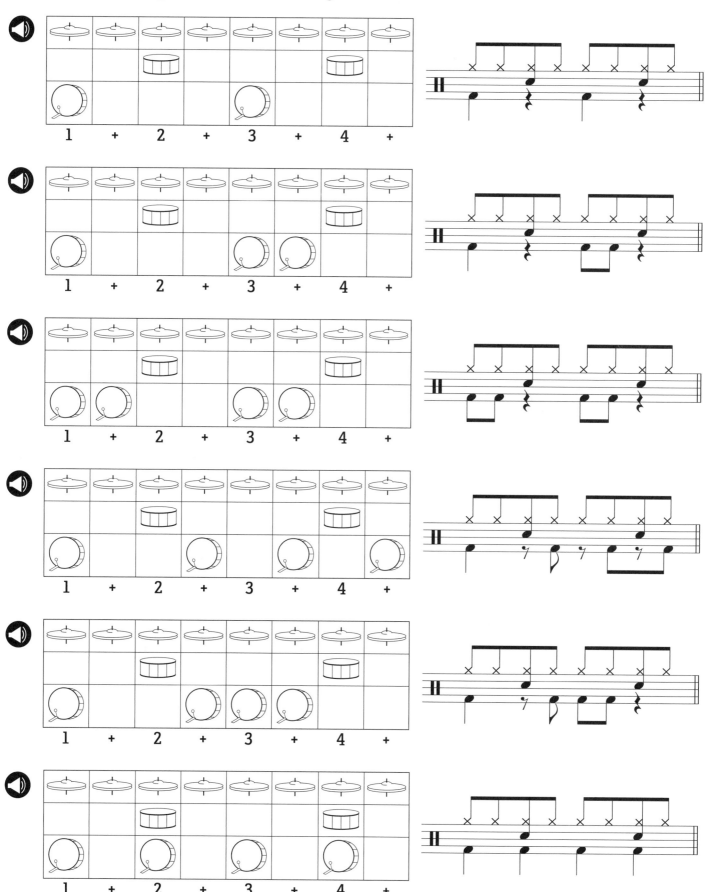

Composition

Your bandmates on guitar, keyboard, and bass are writing riffs and bass lines in this composition activity. When writing drumbeats here, be mindful of the rhythms that they are using and how your drumbeat compliments those rhythms. The drum sounds you choose to use will also affect the compositions. Explore the different tones you can use and pick the ones that you think will sound best:

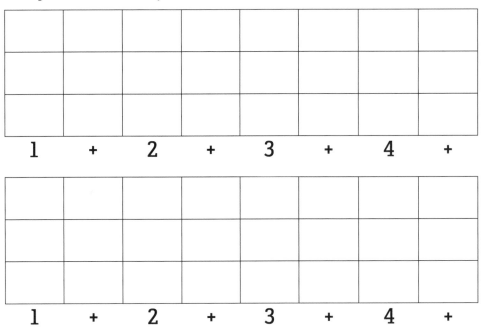

| 1 | + | 2 | + | 3 | + | 4 | + |

| 1 | + | 2 | + | 3 | + | 4 | + |

Playing Drumbeats: Latin Grooves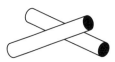

Son Clave

The **son clave** is a common rhythm in Latin and popular music. Its two most common forms are the **2-3** clave and the **3-2** clave. This means that in every two measures of music, there are two groupings of accented beats and upbeats. In 2-3 clave, there is a group of two accented beats within the first measure and three accented points within the next measure. The same goes for 3-2 clave, except the group of three comes before the group of two. You can play the clave rhythms with **claves**, the instruments for which this groove is named:

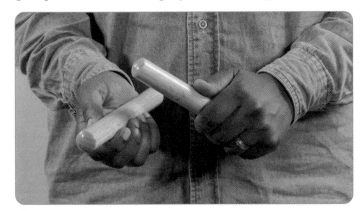

Claves in front

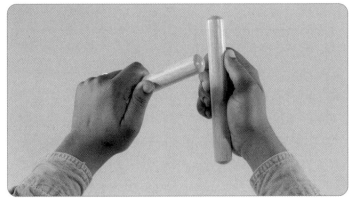

Claves from a player's perspective

Here is the symbol we'll use in our drumbeat diagrams:

You can play clave rhythms on another instrument such as a cymbal or the rim of one of your drums.

2-3 Clave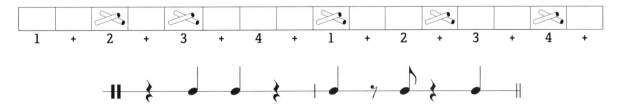

3-2 Clave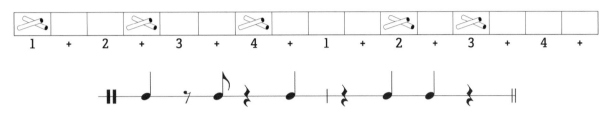

Now, listen to a song like "I Need to Know" by Marc Anthony, find the clave pattern, and try to clap along.

Here are a few other songs that use the clave rhythm in a variety of instruments:
- "Carry Out" by Timbaland ft. Justin Timberlake
- "Pa' la Paloma" by La Sonora Matancera & Celia Cruz
- "Cali Aji" by Grupo Niche

The Guiro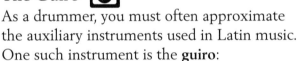

As a drummer, you must often approximate the auxiliary instruments used in Latin music. One such instrument is the **guiro**:

This instrument is played by striking the outer edge with a stick (called a **pua**) and then raking it across the ribbed portion of the outer shell. A typical pattern played on the guiro looks like this:

The guiro isn't featured as a standard piece in the drumset, so drummers will often transfer its rhythms to different parts of the drumset. It's common to play guiro rhythms on the hi-hat in styles such as **salsa** and **conga**:

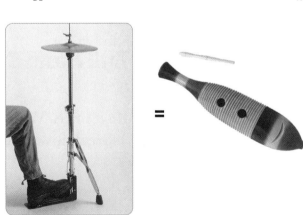

Guiro Rhythms on the Hi-Hat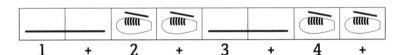

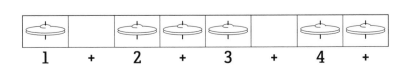
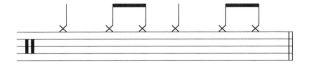

Cumbia Rhythms

Another popular groove is the **cumbia** rhythm, which is featured in songs made famous by artists such as Selena, Juanes, and the Kumbia Kings.

The hi-hat rhythm is similar to the salsa hi-hat rhythm, just twice as fast. The bass drum is also played on all the strong beats, which is called "four on the floor." The cumbia groove is typically played fast, but the overall feeling doesn't venture far from what we have encountered so far. In the next example, play the rhythms twice as fast to give the groove a **double time** feel.

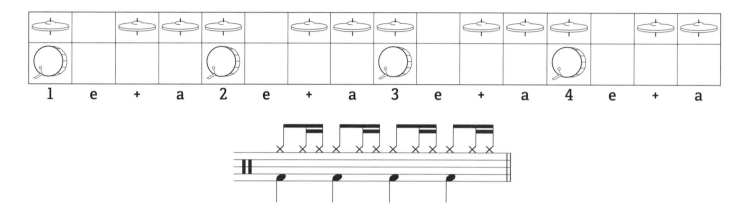

Try playing this groove along with a recording of the song "Bidi Bidi Bom Bom" by Selena.

Instrument Technique: Flams

A **flam** is a rudiment that has a big, full sound, and it is used often in Latin music. Flams can be used to accent something happening in the music and are a fun addition to solos. Flams sound like the word itself: "f-lam." A flam is played by using both sticks—one stick hits the head quietly just before the other hits at a normal volume.

Full Band Song: OYE COMO VA

Santana

Form of Recording: Intro–Verse–Breakdown 1–Verse–Breakdown 1–Verse–Breakdown 1–Verse–Breakdown 2–Verse

For the majority of this tune, you'll want to play this groove. Use your hi-hat to stand in for the guiro!

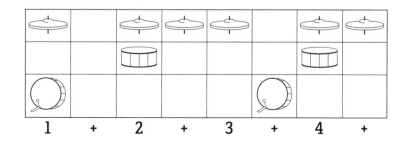

Here's the Breakdown that happens periodically throughout the song. It happens first around the 0:30 mark in the original recording:

Breakdown 1

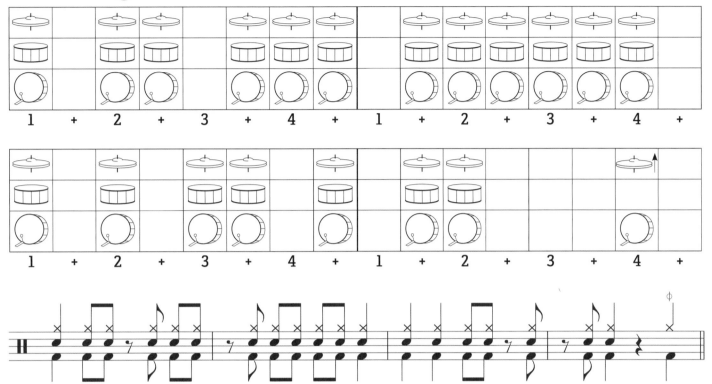

Breakdown 2

The last component in our drumbeats for "Oye Como Va" shows up twice within the song. The first time is around the 2:05 mark in the original recording, where it is played twice. The second time, it is played four times. Be sure to include varied dynamics in this section as you play:

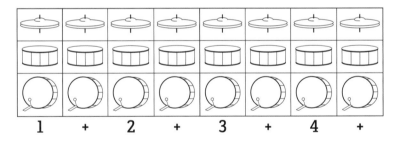

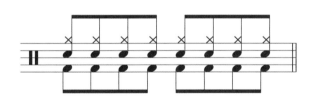

VERSE

Ami   **D**
Oye como va, mi ritmo.

Ami   **D**
Bueno pa gozar, mulata.

Ami   **D**
Oye como va, mi ritmo.

Ami   **D**
Bueno pa gozar, mulata.

Music Theory: Calypso

The **calypso** drumbeat has slightly different rhythms and note placements than many of the previous drumbeats, but it will help lead into the next patterns:

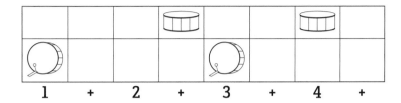 

This drumbeat, though rooted in Caribbean styles of music, has had a major influence on popular music and is used in songs such as "Cheap Thrills" by Sia ft. Sean Paul and "One Dance" by Drake ft. Wizkid & Kyla:

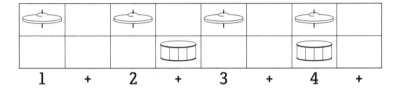 

You can add the kick drum on beats 1 and 3:

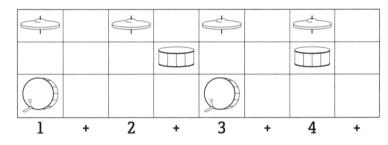 

Think of these drumbeats as being played in double time (counting it twice as fast).

New Techniques: Expanding on Calypso

You can also play this same pattern with open hi-hats on beats 1 and 3 as you play the kick drum:

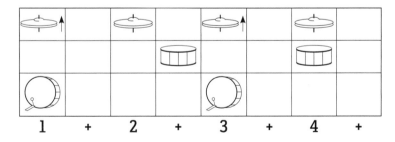 

Instrument Technique: Cross-Stick

Another commonly used technique pertaining to the drums is the cross-stick. Here is the symbol we'll use in our drumbeat diagrams and in standard staff notation:

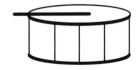

To play a cross-stick, lay your drumstick across the snare drum with about one-third of the stick hanging over the edge. Keeping the tip of the stick on the head of drum, lift it and bring it down against the rim.

Try your favorite drumbeats with a cross-stick instead of a typical snare hit.

Reggaeton/Ska/Rock Steady

A common pattern in **reggaeton** (another name for **reggae**), **ska**, and other Jamaican influenced music is the **one-drop** beat (previously mentioned briefly in Section 4).

This beat has the kick drum and snare playing together on beats 2 and 4:

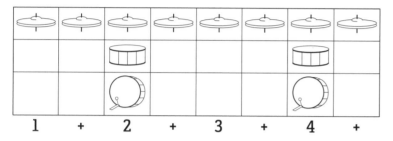

Try playing the one-drop beat on "Waiting in Vain" by Bob Marley & the Wailers:

WAITING IN VAIN
Bob Marley & the Wailers

Music Theory: Accents

To make this beat sound more authentic, you can play **accents** on the upbeats. An accent is when you play slightly louder on a note, making it "pop" within the texture. In standard notation, an accent is represented by this symbol above the note: >

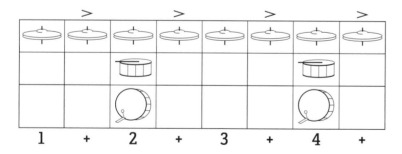

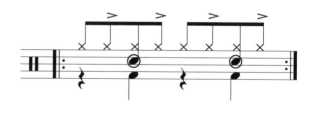

This drumbeat works for other reggae and pop songs too, such as:
- "Is This Love" by Bob Marley & the Wailers
- "With My Own Two Hands" by Ben Harper (You can try this one with cross-stick variations.)
- "One Way Ticket" by Carrie Underwood
- "Do You Really Want to Hurt Me" by Culture Club

Full Band Song: WAKA WAKA (THIS TIME FOR AFRICA)

Shakira

Form of Recording: Intro–Verse–Pre-Chorus–Chorus–Interlude–Verse–Pre-Chorus–Chorus–Bridge–Chorus

"Waka Waka" is a chance to put some of the island grooves you've learned into a Full Band Song. This song uses the calypso beat you learned in its entirety as both an isolated groove and with paired instruments. You'll notice a new symbol called the **sixteenth rest**; it works just like the eighth rest, but for half the value:

Notice that each section uses different combinations of the entire drumbeat:

Rhythm Figure 1

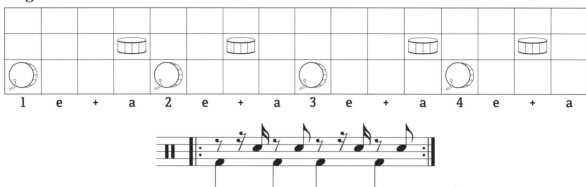

Rhythm Figure 2

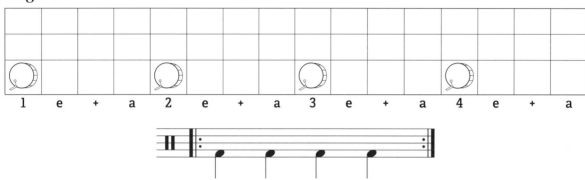

Rhythm Figure 3

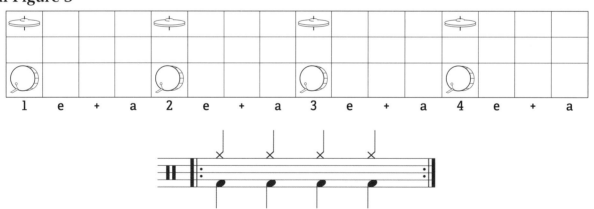

Rhythm Figure 4

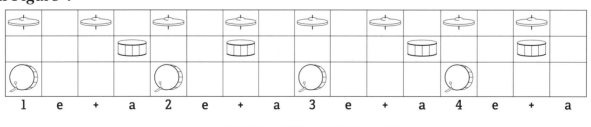

Words and Music by Shakira, Zolani Mahola, John Hill,
Eugene Victor Doo Belley, Jean Ze Bella and Emile Kojidie
Copyright © 2010 Sony/ATV Music Publishing LLC, MyMPM Music, Freshly
Ground, EMI April Music Inc., RodeoMan Music and
Sony/ATV Music Publishing (Germany) Gmbh
All Rights Administered by Sony/ATV Music Publishing LLC,
424 Church Street, Suite 1200, Nashville, TN 37219
International Copyright Secured   All Rights Reserved

VERSE

G   D
You're a good soldier, choosing your battles.

    Emi   C
    Pick yourself up and dust yourself off and get back in the saddle.

G   D
You're on the front line, everyone's watching.

    Emi   C
    You know it's serious, we're getting closer, this isn't over.

G   D   Emi   C
The pressure's on, you feel it. But you got it all, believe it.

PRE-CHORUS

G   D
When you fall get up, oh, oh. And if you fall get up, eh, eh.

    Emi   C
    Tsamina mina zangalewa, 'cause this is Africa.

CHORUS

G   D   Emi   C
Tsamina mina, eh, eh. Waka waka, eh, eh. Tsamina mina zangalewa, this time for Africa.

VERSE

G   D   Emi
Listen to your God. This is our motto. Your time to shine,

        C
    don't wait in line, y vamos por todo.

G   D   Emi
People are raising their expectations. Go on and feed them,

        C
    this is your moment, no hesitation.

G   D   Emi   C
Today's your day, I feel it. You paved the way, believe it.

PRE-CHORUS

G   D
If you get down get up, oh, oh. When you get down get up, eh, eh.

    Emi   C
    Tsamina mina zangalewa, this time for Africa.

BRIDGE

G
Awabuye lamajoni, ipikipiki mama wa A to Z.

Bathi susa lamajoni, ipikipiki mama from East to West.

Bathi waka waka ma eh eh,

Waka waka ma eh eh,

Zonk' izizwe mazibuye, 'cause this is Africa.

SECTION 9

Playing Drumbeats: Funk Drumming

Funk drumming is **syncopated**, or has lots of accented notes that happen between the downbeats. It also uses several types of different sounds. As you'll see in the next section, some of the most popular beats sampled in rap, R&B, and hip-hop music are from funk and soul records made in the 1960s–1980s. In funk music, having a solid grasp of hi-hat technique is crucial to getting a good sound. These types of drumbeats have a mixture of open and closed hi-hat figures.

Warm-Up: Left Hand Freedom

You've practiced being independent with your right foot, now try the same idea with your left hand. To start, play with just your hands, and then add your bass drum on beats 1 and 3. Each drumbeat here is written in either staff notation or in a drumbeat diagram. After playing each drumbeat, rewrite it in standard notation and vice versa:

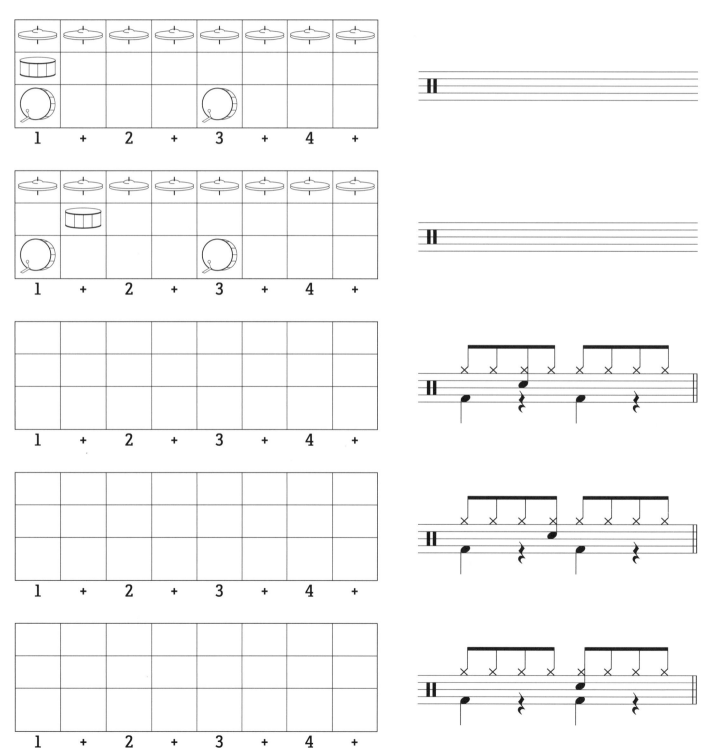

50

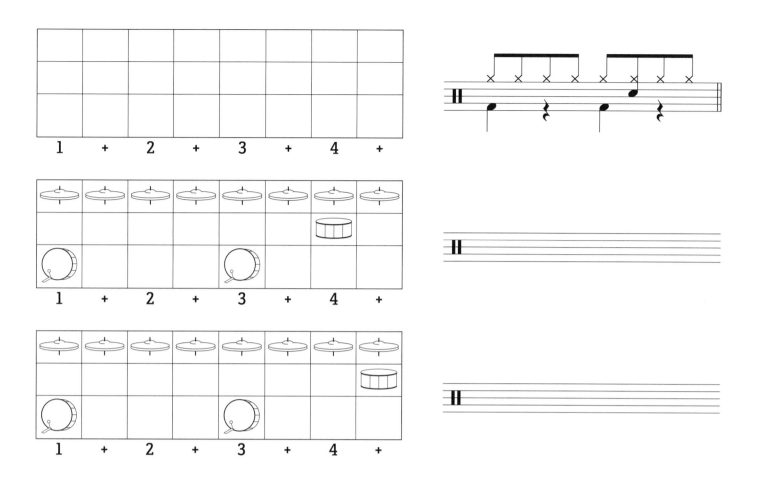

Here are some examples of different snare hits in songs:

TWIST AND SHOUT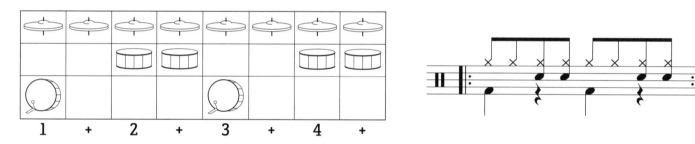
The Beatles

REACH OUT I'LL BE THERE
The Four Tops

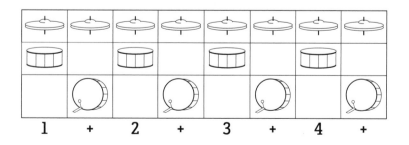

Instrument Skills: Funk Hi-Hat

This beat is used in songs like "Get Up Offa That Thing" by James Brown:

GET UP OFFA THAT THING
James Brown

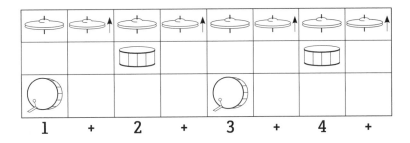
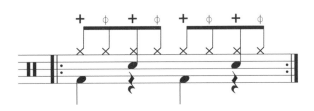

At first glance, it looks like a typical backbeat. However, the hi-hat is going to be what makes this beat sound funkier. Practice it just on its own. Your right hand will still play the same rhythm on each eighth note, but your left foot will lift up on the upbeats and close down on the beats.

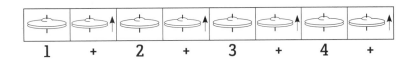
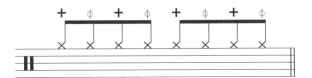

Now, try it all together:

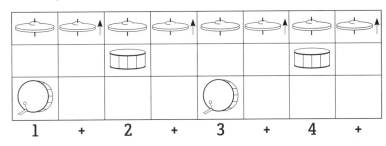

The next example has opened hi-hat only after beats 1 and 3. Notice that the second lift happens at the same time as a bass drum hit. It may help to first learn the groove without the opened hi-hat parts and then add them in later. This beat is used in songs like "Thank You (Falettin Me Be Mice Elf Again)" by Sly and the Family Stone:

THANK YOU (FALETTIN ME BE MICE ELF AGAIN)
Sly and the Family Stone

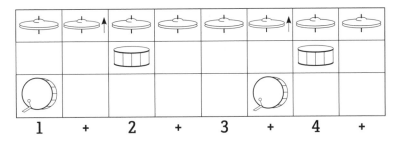

Composition: Verse and Chorus

Now that you know additional drum sounds and grooves, it's time to write more of your own verse and chorus drumbeats. Keep in mind everything you've learned about groove, beat placement, and instrument choices as you write your verse and chorus drumbeats.

Verse

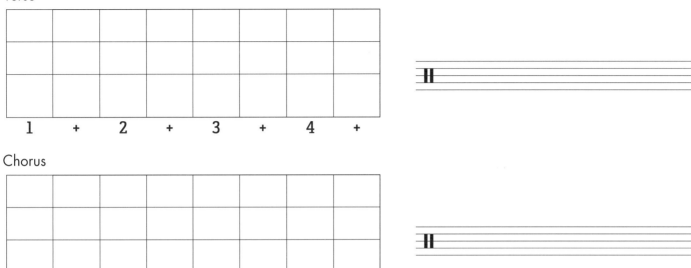

Chorus

Improvisation

This beat is used in songs like "Brown Eyed Girl" by Van Morrison:

BROWN EYED GIRL
Van Morrison

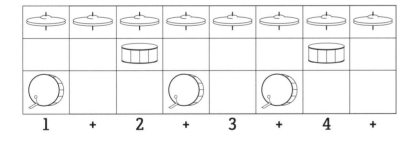

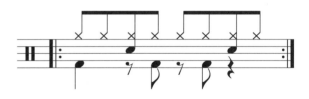

So far, you've mostly accompanied solos for other instruments, meaning the drums have kept the beat while others improvised. Now it's time for your bandmates to accompany you. Take some of the rhythmic soloing ideas from the previous sections, and play them either with the recording or with your bandmates. Here are a few solo ideas for you to try. You can combine them, switch the instrumentation, and extend them to your liking:

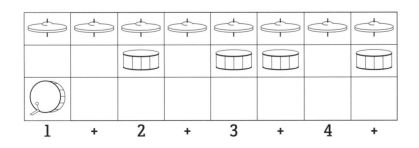

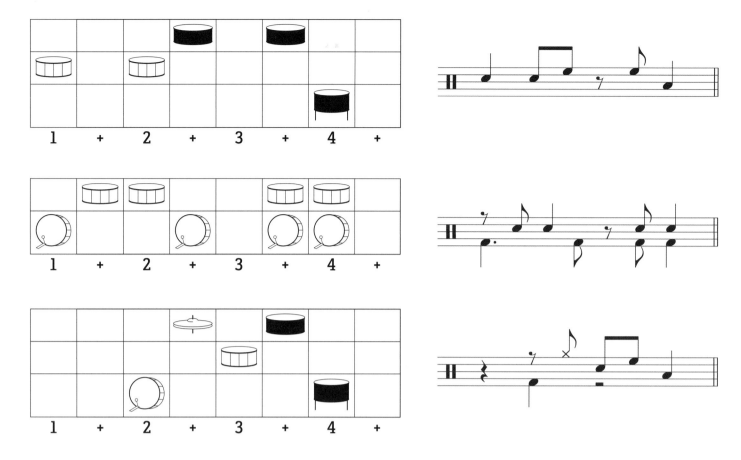

Drums: Choosing the Right Groove

When learning a new tune, you may ask yourself, "What should I play for this song?" Here are some guiding questions to ask when figuring out a drum groove:

- What kinds of instruments do I hear? Which cymbals and drums are playing? Are there other percussion instruments that I might want to emphasize?
- What is the pulse? Clap along to the beat.
- What rhythms are the instruments playing? Play them one at a time, and then write them down to remember for later.
- What is the form of the song?
- What are the dynamics of the song?

Work through the following songs and fill out the blank drumbeat diagrams with new icons if you want to change the instrumentation:

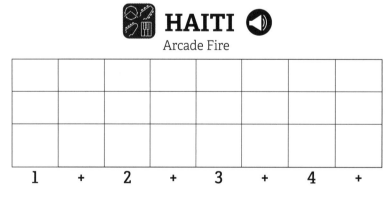

Options

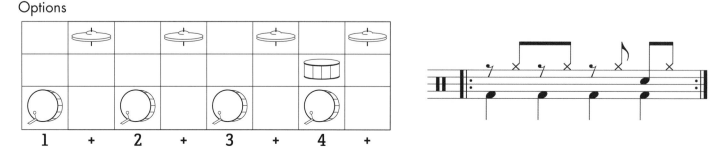

WILD THING

The Troggs

1	+	2	+	3	+	4	+

Options

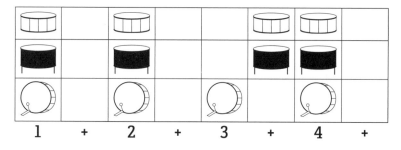

THE EDGE OF GLORY

Lady Gaga

1	+	2	+	3	+	4	+

Options

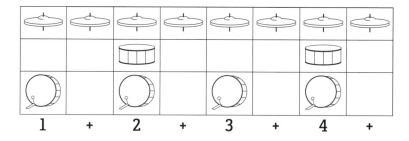

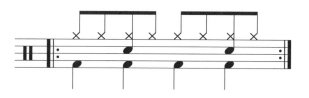

Here are three more songs your bandmates are working on:

HALO

Beyoncé

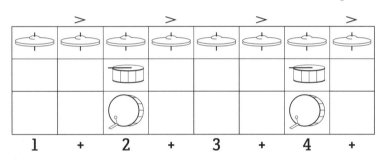

WAITING IN VAIN

Bob Marley & the Wailers

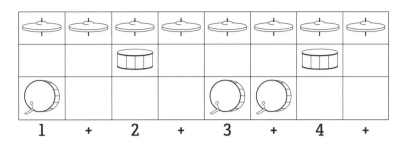

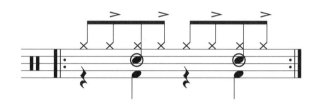

HEY THERE DELILAH

Plain White T's

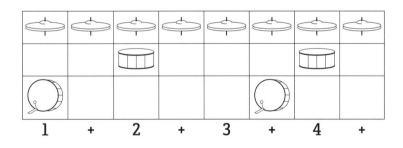

Full Band Song: BEST DAY OF MY LIFE

American Authors

Form of Recording: Intro–Verse–Pre-Chorus–Chorus–Verse–Pre-Chorus–Chorus–Bridge–Chorus

This Full Band Song is not so funky, so you can either play it just as you hear in the recording, or you can ask your bandmates if they want to try to play it funky. The Chorus might be a great time to substitute the groove from "Get Up Offa That Thing." We've included simplified grooves to get you started.

The instrumentation slowly changes during this song. Can you listen and figure out when each part occurs? If you want to try your own version, then try substituting other instruments. For example, you could play the floor tom instead of the bass drum at the beginning, or rim clicks instead of the hi-hat.

Suggested Grooves:

Verse

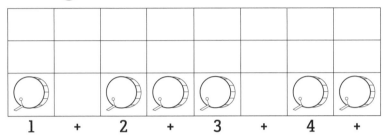

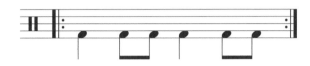

Pre-Chorus

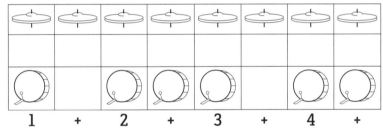

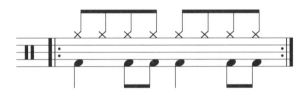

Chorus 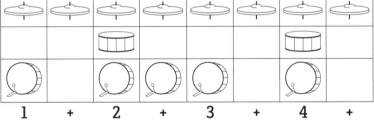 (Don't forget to play a crash at the beginning of this section.)

Bridge

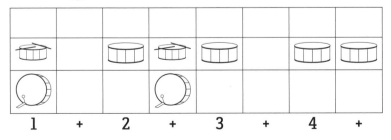

VERSE

D
I had a dream so big and loud. I jumped so high I touched the clouds.

G
Whoa-o-o-o-o-oh. Whoa-o-o-o-o-oh.

D
I stretched my hands out to the sky. We danced with monsters through the night.

G
Whoa-o-o-o-o-oh. Whoa-o-o-o-o-oh.

PRE-CHORUS

D   **Emi**
I'm never gonna look back, whoa. I'm never gonna give it up, no. Please don't wake me now.

CHORUS

D   **G**
Wo-o-o-o-oo! This is gonna be the best day of my life, my life.

D   **G**
Wo-o-o-o-oo! This is gonna be the best day of my life, my life.

VERSE

D
I howled at the moon with friends. And then the sun came crashing in.

G
Whoa-o-o-o-o-oh. Whoa-o-o-o-o-oh.

      D
But all the possibilities, no limits just epiphanies.

G
Whoa-o-o-o-o-oh. Whoa-o-o-o-o-oh.

BRIDGE

D
I hear it calling outside my window.

I feel it in my soul, soul.

The stars were burning so bright,

The sun was out 'til midnight.

I say we lose control, control.

SECTION 10

Section 10 primarily looks at hip-hop music. You can use a lot of the drumbeats that we discussed earlier, but with some modifications to fit the style.

Beatboxing

Try beatboxing the beat below, using a "buh" sound for the bass and a "kah" sound for the snare:

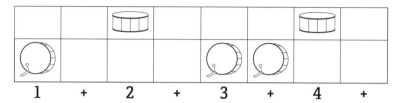

This beat is used in songs such as "Kick, Push" by Lupe Fiasco. We'll cover this Full Band Song later in the section, but here are the isolated drums to get you started:

KICK, PUSH
Lupe Fiasco

Now, try it on the drumset. This drumbeat has a bass drum pattern based from the one you just beatboxed but has additional elements.

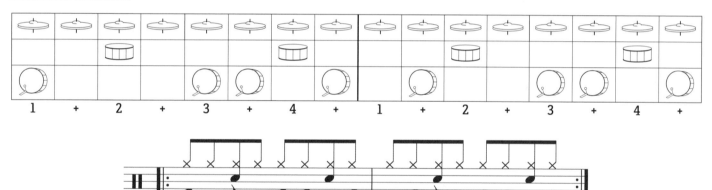

Music History: Sampling

Try playing this beat from "Ham and Eggs" by A Tribe Called Quest:

HAM AND EGGS
A Tribe Called Quest

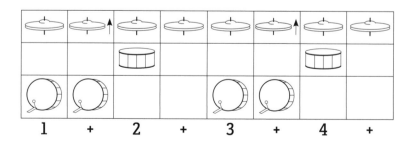

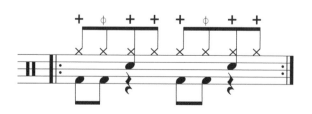

This song uses **sampling** to make the instrumental track. A Tribe Called Quest used parts of three funky tracks from the early 1970s and put them together. Afterwards, they added singing and rapping over the top. The drum part of this tune comes from a song called "We've Gotta Find a Way Back to Love" by Freda Payne. Try playing the same beat over that tune.

59

Things to notice about the sample:
- You can hear both a drumset and bongos from that track.
- A Tribe Called Quest slightly slowed the drum track down.
- Because A Tribe Called Quest used only a small part of the track, there is less variation in fills, hi-hat openings, and other parts within their song. Hip-hop beats tend to stay very consistent throughout much of the song when they're made using samples.

Instrument Technique: Soloing with a Bass Drum Groove

We have spent a lot of time accompanying other instruments while they solo. Drummers can also accompany their own solos. Try keeping a simple bass drum pattern going like this one:

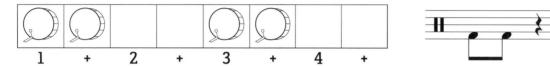

You can also play the bass drum only on beats 1 and 3 for a different sound. Now, try to keep that going while you play some different combinations of quarter notes and eighth notes on the rest of the kit. Start with whatever comes to mind, and then try a few of these patterns, which are similar to the ones you've played before:

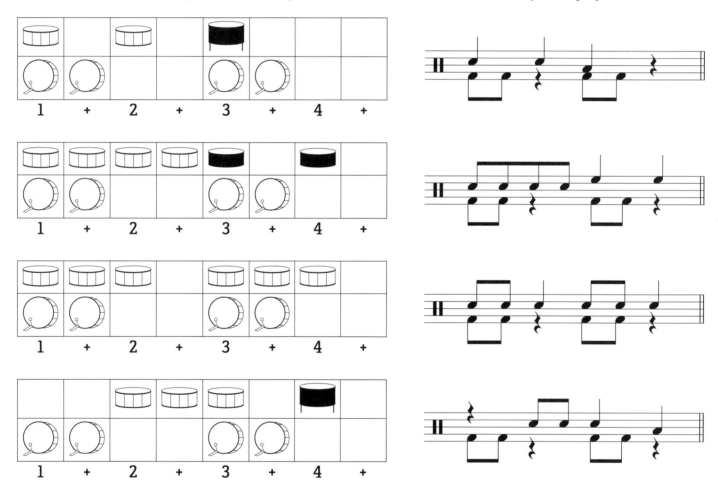

Over the course of a solo, adding these elements in slowly will make it more exciting. Try starting with no bass drum, and then adding it on beats 1 and 3.

Combining a bass drum groove with a solo takes some time, so keep at it. You will have a chance to practice soloing (with or without a bass drum groove) over the next Full Band Song.

Instrument Technique: Exploring More Sounds

Try these sounds out. You can play them on their own, and then put them into a drumbeat.

Cross-Stick Flam

You've played a cross-stick and a flam before. Now, put them together to play a **cross-stick flam**. Here is the symbol we'll use in our drumbeat diagram:

When you play a cross-stick flam, hit the top of the stick you're holding in your left hand with the other stick:

Since you won't be able to play the hi-hat at the same time, your beat might look like this:

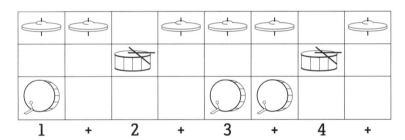
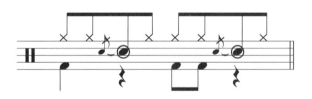

Rimshot

A **rimshot** can produce a very loud sound without using a lot of energy. To play this, hit the rim and the head of the drum at the same time with one stick. It takes a lot of practice to make a rimshot sound consistent each time, so keep practicing it for when you have a chance to be loud.

Cymbal Sounds

Cymbals are one of the most personal things to a drummer, as they can produce a wide variety of tones. All these sounds are very specific, so you probably won't want to use them all the time.

Sizzle Sounds: You can use paper clips, a chain, or even clear tape and a penny/nickel to make the cymbal ring out and "sizzle" for a long time. Make sure you get permission first to do this on any cymbal that doesn't belong to you.

Broken Cymbals: Do you know someone who has a broken cymbal laying around? Don't let them throw it away! Broken cymbals can be great for getting sizzle sounds of their own or stacking with other cymbals. However, don't break a cymbal on purpose! Try some of those sounds on this next drumbeat, which can be played with songs like "My House" by Flo Rida:

MY HOUSE
Flo Rida

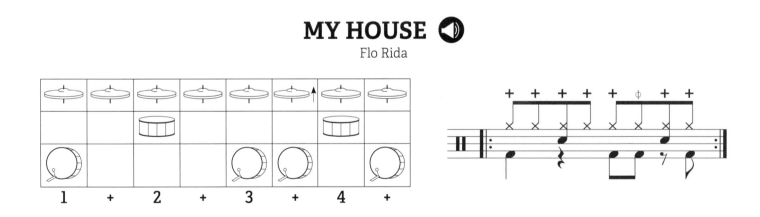

Note—In the original recording, the last bass drum hit happens only sometimes, often at the end of a phrase of four or eight measures. Listen carefully to hear the pattern.

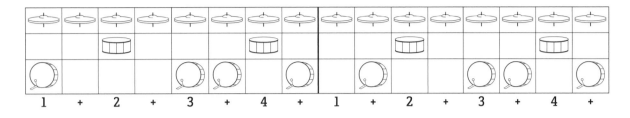

Full Band Song: KICK, PUSH

Lupe Fiasco

Form of Recording: Verse–Chorus–Verse–Chorus–Verse–Chorus

Earlier in this section, we covered the basic drumbeat for "Kick, Push." You can play that beat again over the full track, but see if you can figure out where the extra kick drum is placed within the groove. (Hint—listen for the change around beat 3 of every measure.)

VERSE

First got it when he was six, didn't know any tricks. Matter fact,

First time he got on it he slipped, landed on his hip and bust his lip.

For a week he had to talk with a lisp, like this.

Now we can end the story right here,

But shorty didn't quit, it was something in the air, yea.

He said it was somethin' so appealing. He couldn't fight the feelin'.

Somethin' about it, he knew he couldn't doubt it, couldn't understand it,

Brand it, since the first kickflip he landed, uh. Labeled a misfit, abandoned,

Ca-kunk, ca-kunk, kunk. His neighbors couldn't stand it, so he was banished to the park.

Started in the morning, wouldn't stop till after dark, yea.

When they said "it's getting late in here, so I'm sorry young man, there's no skating here."

CHORUS

So we kick, push, kick, push, kick, push, kick, push, coast.

And the way he roll just a rebel to the world with no place to go.

So we kick, push, kick, push, kick, push, kick, push, coast.

So come and skate with me, just a rebel looking for a place to be.

So let's kick, and push, and coast.

Words and Music by Wasalu Jaco and Rudolph Loyola Lopez
Copyright © 2006 by Universal Music - Careers, Heavy As Heaven Music, Universal Music - MGB Songs, 1st And 15th Publishing and Mr. Lopez Music
All Rights for Heavy As Heaven Music Administered by Universal Music - Careers
All Rights for 1st And 15th Publishing and Mr. Lopez Music Administered by Universal Music - MGB Songs
International Copyright Secured   All Rights Reserved

VERSE

Uh, uh, uh. My man got a lil' older, became a better roller (yea).

No helmet, hell-bent on killin' himself, was what his momma said.

But he was feelin' himself, got a lil' more swagger in his style.

Met his girlfriend, she was clappin' in the crowd.

Love is what was happening to him now, uh. He said "I would marry you but I'm engaged to
These aerials and varials, and I don't think this board is strong enough to carry two."

She said "beau, I weigh 120 pounds. Now, lemme make one thing clear, I don't need to ride
yours, I got mine right here." So she took him to a spot he didn't know about,

Somewhere in the apartment parking lot, she said, "I don't normally take dates in here."

Security came and said, "I'm sorry there's no skating here."

CHORUS

So they kick, push, kick, push, kick, push, kick, push, coast.

And the way they roll, just lovers intertwined with no place to go.

And so they kick, push, kick, push, kick, push, kick, push, coast.

So come and skate with me, just a rebel looking for a place to be.

So let's kick, and push, and coast.

VERSE

Yea uh, yea, yea. Before he knew he had a crew that wasn't no punk

In they Spitfire shirts and SB Dunks. They would push, till they couldn't skate no more.

Office buildings, lobbies wasn't safe no more.

And it wasn't like they wasn't getting chased no more,

Just the freedom is better than breathing, they said.

An escape route, they used to escape out when things got crazy they needed to break out.

(They'd head) to any place with stairs, and good grinds the world was theirs, uh.

And they four wheels would take them there,

Until the cops came and said, "There's no skating here."

CHORUS

So they kick, push, kick, push, kick, push, kick, push, coast.

And the way they roll, just rebels without a cause with no place to go.

And so they kick, push, kick, push, kick, push, kick, push, coast.

So come roll with me, just a rebel looking for a place to be.

So let's kick, and push, and coast.

SECTION 11

Instrument Technique: Combining Bass and Snare Drum Freedom

Here are some exercises that combine the snare and bass drum in different patterns along with a constant eighth-note rhythm played on the hi-hat:

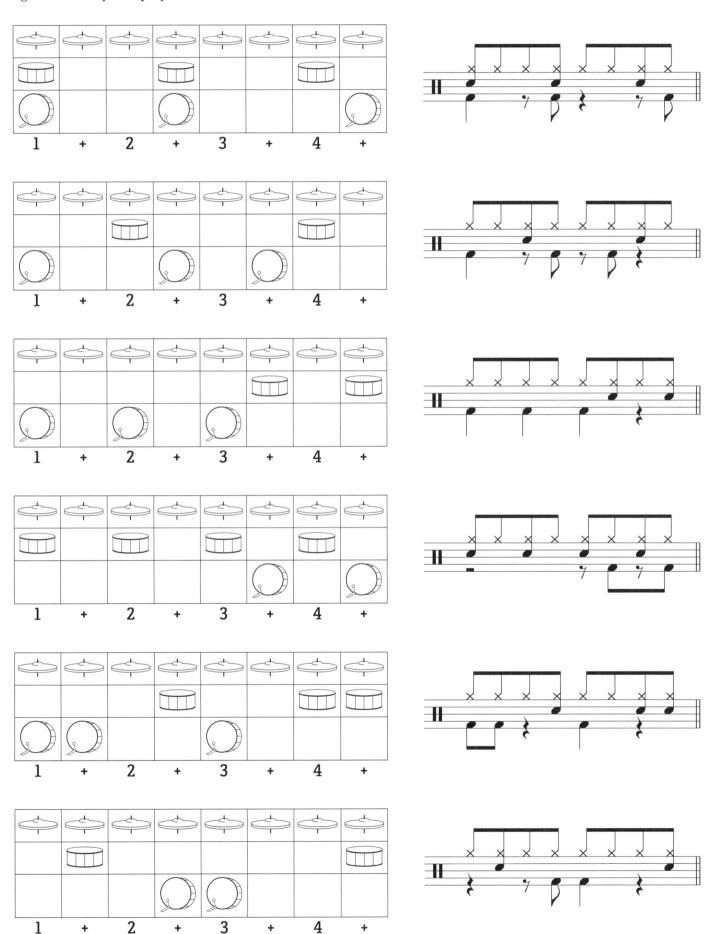

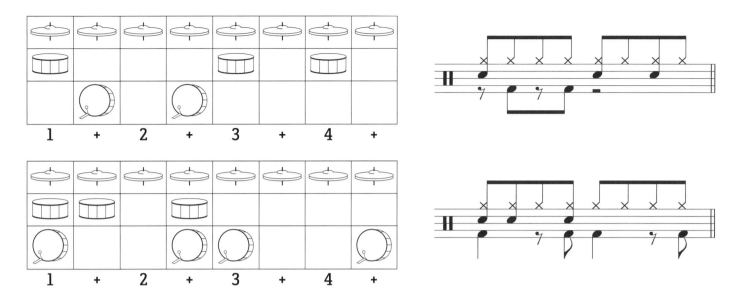

Make up some more combinations on your own, and write them in the diagrams below:

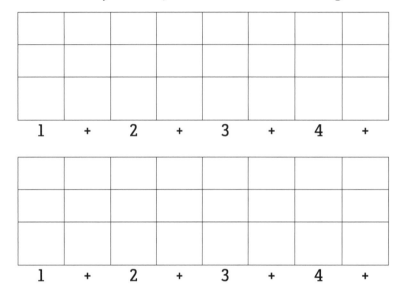

Music Theory: Choosing the Right Drum Groove

Here are a few more songs to transcribe and create beats for:

GIVE ME ONE REASON 🔊
Tracy Chapman

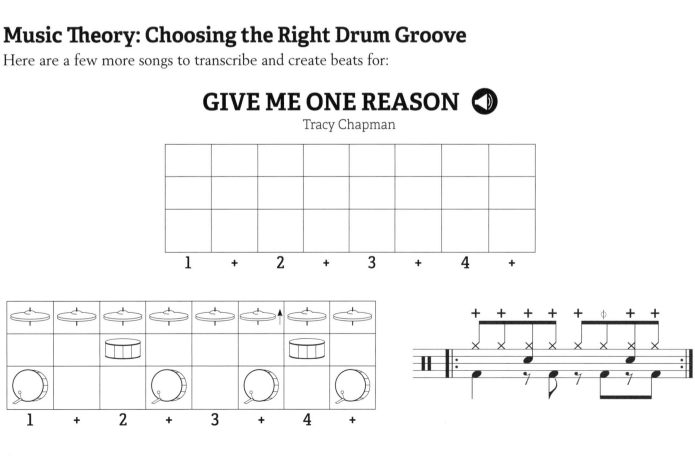

SÚBEME LA RADIO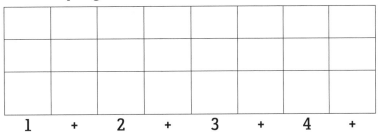

Enrique Iglesias ft. Descemer Bueno, Zion & Lennox

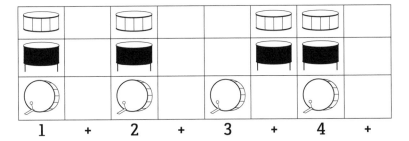

This last example does not feature a typical backbeat, so carefully count along:

WILD THING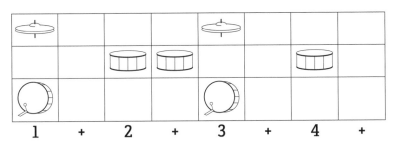

The Troggs

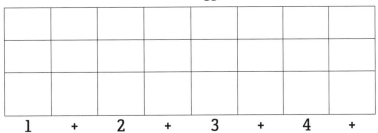

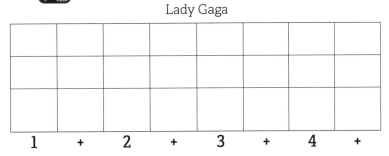

THE EDGE OF GLORY

Lady Gaga

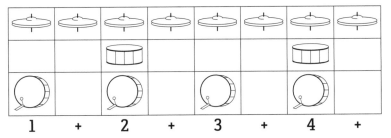

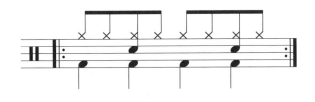

Full Band Song: UMBRELLA 🔊
Rihanna

Form of Recording: Intro–Verse–Chorus–Verse–Chorus–Bridge–Chorus

The drumbeat in this song doesn't change much throughout. However, you can add fills and crash hits, but keep them appropriate within the song. Fills are a great way to create movement between sections, and they help the listener know when a new section has arrived.

Most of the sections in this song are eight measures long. So you can play the main beat of the song seven times, and then add a fill into the last measure. That might be a one-, two-, three-, or four-beat fill, depending on how you and your bandmates determine what best fits the music. We've simplified the drumbeats in the notated examples, but if you're feeling adventurous, try to play the full version using sixteenth-note rhythms.

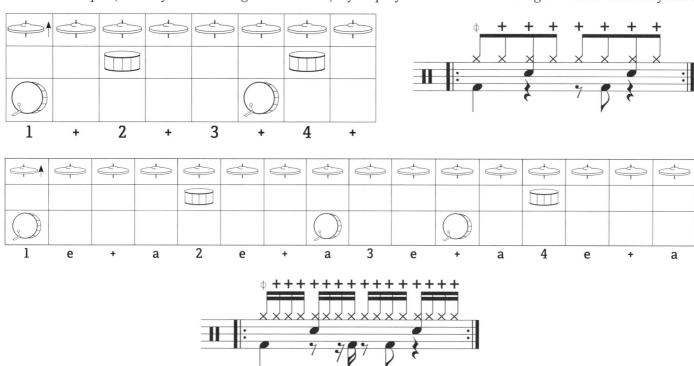

Don't forget that you can always compose your own drum fills. Here are some blank diagrams that you can use to write out your own ideas:

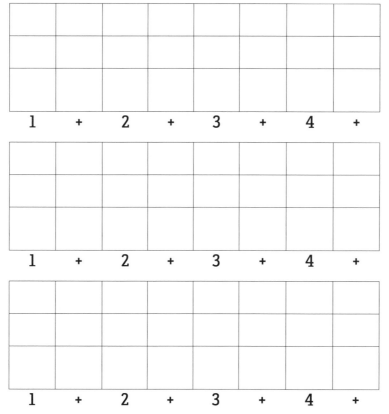

VERSE

Gb5
You have my heart, and we'll never be worlds apart.
                                                Ab5

           F5   Bb5
Maybe in magazines, but you'll still be my star.

           Gb5   Ab5
Baby, 'cause in the dark you can't see shiny cars.

                 F5   Bb5
And that's when you need me there, with you I'll always share, because...

CHORUS

Gb5   Db5   Ab5
When the sun shines, we'll shine together. Told you I'd be here forever.

               Bb5
Said I'll always be your friend. Took an oath, I'mma stick it out 'til the end.

Gb5   Db5   Ab5
Now that it's raining more than ever, know that we'll still have each other.

               Bb5   Gb5
You can stand under my umbrella. You can stand under my umbrella.

         Db5   Ab5
(Ella, ella, eh, eh, eh.) Under my umbrella.

         Bb5   Gb5
(Ella, ella, eh, eh, eh.) Under my umbrella.

         Db5   Ab5
(Ella, ella, eh, eh, eh.) Under my umbrella.

         Bb5
(Ella, ella, eh, eh, eh, eh, eh, eh.)

VERSE

           Gb5   Ab5
These fancy things, will never come in between.

               F5   Bb5
You're part of my entity, here for infinity.

           Gb5   Ab5
When the war has took its part, when the world has dealt its cards,

   F5   Bb5
If the hand is hard, together we'll mend your heart.

BRIDGE

Cb5   Gb5
You can run into my arms. It's OK, don't be alarmed.

     Db5   Ab5
Come here to me. There's no distance in between our love.

Cb5   Gb5
So go on and let the rain pour.

               F5
I'll be all you need and more, because...

Form of Recording: Intro–Verse–Chorus–Verse–Chorus–Bridge/Outro

This song will include several of the topics we've covered in the book: changing instruments on the drumset, playing the crash on beat 1, adding fills, open and closed hi-hat figures, and changing kick drum patterns.

Intro Fill

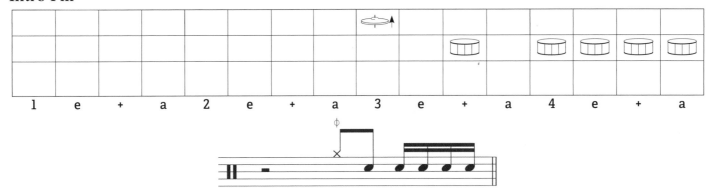

Play this drumbeat eight times:

Verse

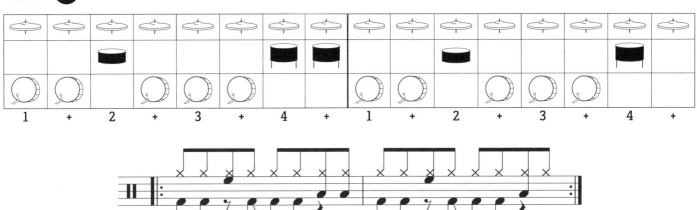

Then play this pattern, with the fill starting on beat 3:

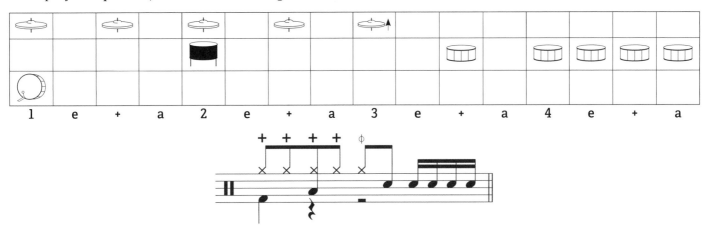

The Chorus is a repeated two-measure drumbeat. Play the hi-hat open:

Chorus

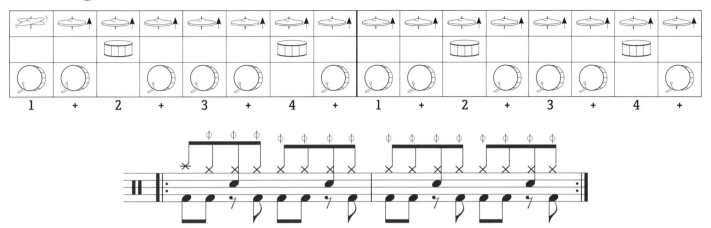

Bridge/Outro

You can use the same pattern that you played on the Verse for the Outro.

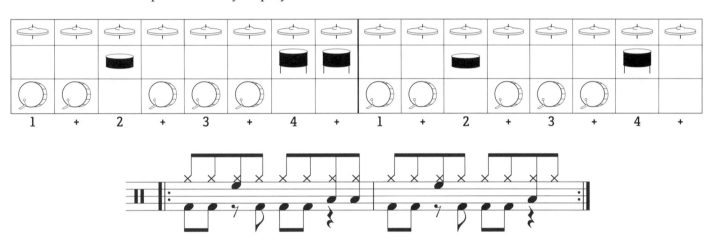

VERSE

Emi   Cmaj7   G   D
Another head hangs lowly, child is slowly taken.

Emi   Cmaj7   G   D
And the violence caused such silence. Who are we mistaken?

           Emi   Cmaj7   G   D
But you see it's not me, it's not my family. In your head, in your head they are fighting,

            Emi   Cmaj7
With their tanks, and their bombs, and their bombs, and their guns.

        G   D
In your head, in your head they are crying.

CHORUS

          E5   C5   G5   D5
In your head, in your head, zombie, zombie, zombie, hey, hey.

              E5   C5   G5   D5
What's in your head, in your head, zombie, zombie, zombie, hey, hey, hey?

VERSE

Emi   Cmaj7   G   D
Another mother's breakin' heart is taking over.

Emi   Cmaj7   G   D
When the violence causes silence, we must be mistaken.

           Emi   Cmaj7   G   D
It's the same old theme since nineteen-sixteen. In your head, in your head they're still fighting,

            Emi   Cmaj7
With their tanks, and their bombs, and their bombs, and their guns.

        G   D
In your head, in your head they are dying.

CHORUS

          E5   C5   G5   D5
In your head, in your head, zombie, zombie, zombie, hey, hey.

              E5   C5   G5   D5
What's in your head, in your head, zombie, zombie, zombie. Hey, hey, hey?